POWER,
PRESIDENTS,
AND
PROFESSORS

POWER, PRESIDENTS, AND PROFESSORS

NICHOLAS J. DEMERATH
RICHARD W. STEPHENS
R. ROBB TAYLOR

BASIC BOOKS, INC., *Publishers*

NEW YORK • LONDON

378.11
D 376

PREFACE

IN 1954 THE AUTHORS, then at the University of North
Carolina, began their studies of organizational behavior in
universities. This book is a result. As my collaborators' former professor, writing in India, where to be older is to be
privileged, I have chosen to do our preface. And I wish to
acknowledge first not only the work of Professor Stephens
and Dr. Taylor, but also to thank them for tolerating the
mayhem I have committed on their monographs, which provide the basis for much of the book.

For the financial and other assistance we required, we are
indebted to the Organizational Research Group of the Institute for Research in Social Science at the University of North
Carolina, as well as to the Social Science Institute of Washington University at St. Louis. In these connections we think
of Mr. Luigi Petrullo, of the Navy; Dr. Bernard Berelson,
then at the Ford Foundation's late, lamented Behavioral
Sciences Division; my partner in the direction of the Organization Research Group, Professor John W. Thibaut; the director
of the Institute for Research in Social Sciences, Gordon W.
Blackwell, then a professor, more recently a university president. Dr. Taylor's survey of thirty academic departments at
five major universities was indispensably aided by Professor
Theodore Caplow (then at the University of Minnesota), who
employed Taylor in his own work.

The study of administrative style at the University of North

Carolina began in 1956 with a survey for a faculty committee to which I belonged and which Dr. Taylor assisted. Then, having repeated the survey in 1960, with the help of Professors Alexander Heard (now chancellor of Vanderbilt University), W. C. Robson, James L. Godfrey, William Wells, and other friends at North Carolina, we were able to complete a longitudinal study of the effects of administrative change on a university faculty—a rare sort of study. No less unusual was the action of the chancellor of the University, William Aycock, who permitted us to identify the organization we observed.

We are indebted also to my associates at Washington University at St. Louis who suffered my mistakes as an administrator over six years, not in one but two jobs; and then in 1962 welcomed me back to the collegial fold as a "pure," if peripatetic, professor and gave me the time to write. To Professor Joseph A. Kahl goes our gratitude for encouragement, criticism, and statistical help. To Mrs. Dorothy Altheimer, Miss Marilyn Harrington, and their office mates at the Social Science Institute, we are grateful for typing and editorial assistance.

Most recently, my collaborators and I are obligated to colleagues in the Ford Foundation (India) who aided the completion of the book; especially to Dr. Malcolm Willey, Dr. Jason Finkle, and my secretary and typist, Mrs. Hazel Dias.

Finally, personal kudos to my wife, Helen, and our children for all the things authors conventionally mention; plus my good fortune in a namesake whose sociological writings are sometimes mistakenly attributed to me!

NICHOLAS J. DEMERATH

New Delhi
July 1966

CONTENTS

PART IV

The Academic Departments: Power and Reputation

PART V

Implications

PART I

Introduction

1

The Why and How of the Book

As PUNDITS of administration often observe, the American university is a most peculiar kind of organization. Its goals are unclear. Its products are intangible and non-measurable. It seems to pay little attention to the demands of its customers. It has two lines of authority, the bureaucratic and the professional, both tending to be blurred and diffused. Its best employees, the most distinguished professors, are often disloyal to the organization. And there isn't much that "top management" can do about these things directly—and still have a university of excellence. A peculiar kind of organization, yes. But why is it peculiar? Why should it be so unlike the well-managed business, government agency, army, or industry? What is good administration for professional and creative people? How can the requisites of organization and the needs of academicians be accommodated? These and more particular questions, to be introduced later, have prompted our inquiries.

Our book is about American universities viewed as managed organizations. Unlike most observers of higher education, we are not concerned directly with teaching and learning. It is the administration of universities seen sociologically that concerns us. Educational affairs in the usual sense—be they curricular or extracurricular—are outside our ken. We even go so far as to regard students not as members of universities but as one of several clienteles we choose to put to one side as far as our studies are concerned. But this is not to say we are unconcerned with the process of education. On the contrary, we seek knowledge of certain organizational and administrative phenomena that are critical elements of the university as it has evolved in the United States. Especially important are the phenomena of power in the human relationships of faculties and administrators, trustees and presidents. And power's importance is traceable, not only to the theories of sociologists, but to the contemporary situation of the university in the United States.

Background Problem: The Jeopardy of the University

The university's main mission has been to nurture the mind and the spirit of man—be the man freshman or professor, artist or scientist, here or there in space or time. Broad humanistic training, religious indoctrination, preservation of the past, discovery and extension of knowledge, the creation of aristocratic or administrative elites—all these goals of the university, in their time and turn, have necessitated cultivation of the intellect and of attitudes and emotions. This the university has done by providing the environments and facilities for various combinations of thought, action, and—last but not least—meditation. Of necessity, the elements and the organization of such an enterprise are unique, comparable only

4

to some ecclesiastical organizations, large "teaching" hospitals, and basic-research laboratories.

Though nurture of mind and of spirit has been the main mission of the university since the thirteenth century, both the institution and its mission are in jeopardy today. Vastly different societal demands are pressed, which the university may be unable to meet; or, if met, may destroy the central intellectual and creative capacities of the university. There will be twice as many young people at the end of the next ten years, and Americans have already come to regard a "college education" as an egalitarian right, a middle-class ritual, and a doorway to the most appealing occupations. They think of the university as the principal source and ratifier for every craft that wants to be known as a "profession." At the same time, the university is expected to produce more and more skilled manpower to make discoveries, design hardware, and operate new technologies, which are desired no matter the social costs. If the college and the university could meet all these demands merely by transmitting present knowledge, the educational task would be comparatively simple. But the future compels intellectual as well as technological change. It is a future for which preparation is not easy. Accordingly, instead of passing along learned lumber and presuming to offer "complete education," the university must do what is more difficult: equip young people with the motivation, the values, and the skills for continuous intellectual inquiry, responsible action, and personal growth; and also transmit ever-changing knowledge. To do this, the university itself must be continually changing.

Different, historically, are still other demands made of the university today, demands we need only mention. The demand for research and development is already enormous, and is still increasing, particularly in the physical and biological sciences and in engineering. One observer has alluded in nutritional terms to some dangerous imbalances in the university: "Hu-

5

manistic research and creativity subsist marginally on a very thin diet. Social science research is putting on a little weight."[1] There has been a great increase in the demand for international services. These include the training of foreign nationals in the United States and abroad, the planning and staffing of numerous and varied institutions and programs for the "underdeveloped" countries, and the conduct of research in support of these and other international services. The impact of these activities has been felt in almost every university department, academic and business, and especially, perhaps, in the foreign-language departments. Finally, there is the older but scarcely lessened demand for mass entertainment— by means of big-time athletics especially, whose corrosive influences are decried by most educators.

These demands the university cannot meet or resolve with present resources of manpower, facilities, and money. Although new educational methods, different organizational forms, and more faculty are required, higher salaries and larger budgets for plant and equipment are indispensable parts of the solution. The universities and the public have yet to devise the channels by which more adequate financing of the country's academic future may be assured. In this connection, it is worth noting that a prime source of funds has become a competitor. The American corporations are now spending more each year on educating their employees than the combined budgets of all American colleges and universities. Many of these rapidly expanding educational or training activities do not belong in universities, but some of them do. In any case, they are fifty-two per cent financed at federal expense, through the corporate tax structure, while the debate over federal support to education continues.[2]

[1] Philip H. Coombs, "The University and Its External Environment," in George H. Daigneault (ed.), *The Changing University* (Chicago: Center for the Study of Liberal Education for Adults, 1959), p. 27.
   [2] *Ibid.*, p. 26.

6

How near the American university will come to meeting these great expectations will depend on how the American people will allocate their wealth; on the value they will attach to mental nurture, excellence, and creativity in contrast to consumer comforts, pleasures, and conformity. But, though the future of the American university depends on the larger society, it depends in great part also on the faculties, the administrators, and the trustees of universities. They, after all, are the principal custodians of the values they espouse. That university members have done so little to further needed educational legislation in the Congress in recent years has been a complaint of those close to the Washington scene. This may be but one symptom, however, of a rather general institutional sickness. Paul Lazarsfeld, in his 1962 presidential address to the American Sociological Association, described a crippling malaise of our universities in these terms:

. . . we witness a dangerous divergence: academic freedom is more and more interpreted in such a way as to keep the administration out of any truly academic affairs; and the faculty, in turn, has come to consider administration beneath its dignity. But educational innovations are, by definition, intellectual as well as administrative tasks. And so, they have fallen into a no-man's land: the president and his staff wait for the faculty to take the initiative; the professors on their side consider that such matters would take time away from their true scholarly pursuits. As a result, many of our universities have a dangerously low level of institutional development.[3]

Others have viewed with alarm the destruction of social environments suited to the needs of creative individuals, not the least of these being the universities. The distinguished physicist P. W. Bridgman of Harvard once said that the maintenance of settings for creativity in our large and complex universities and laboratories may be one of the greatest problems of our time. Certainly the university is no longer "a

[3] Paul F. Lazarsfeld, "The Sociology of Empirical Social Research," *American Sociological Review*, XXVII (December 1962), 764.

community of scholars" in the ancient sense; nor is there any likelihood of a return to the earlier collegial form, character- ized by small, multi-bonded groups of teachers and students who were informally controlled and motivated by clear and gen- erally known systems of rewards based on scholarly achieve- ment. Increasing size, greater specialization, and the pervasive managerial norms and forms of business and government have all combined to make our universities managed organizations, and, however unique or peculiar they may be as organizations, they are no doubt less unlike the modern corporation or government agency than their European and early American prototypes were. Thus, many faculty members, all too keenly aware of these developments and of what is at stake, become anti-organization, anti-administration "keepers of the flame." Too often they do not know, or dare not admit, that most con- texts of inquiry and mental nurture must, in our day, be planned and protected if they are to exist at all. The activism and absence of leisure, the hustle for success and status, the noise and nuisance of mass society outside the university, and the "geese in the forum" within—all these things poison the soil in which creativity flourishes. Moreover, settings for men- tal nurture and creativity must be organized deliberately and administered appropriately with faculty participation in the planning and policy-making. The "low level" of faculty- guided institutional development to which Lazarsfeld referred is dangerous indeed.

Such are the facts and the considerations that make the study of power and administrative behavior in our universities more than a purely scholarly endeavor. Though much is writ- ten and said about higher education and academic institutions, there have been few systematic empirical studies of university organization and management. It has been remarked more than once that university professors know more about every- thing else than they know about themselves and their habitat. The human organizations of industry, unions, government, restaurants, hospitals, prisons, armies, political parties, and gangs have been investigated in numerous instances and by various methods. These studies—variously labeled organizational analysis, administrative behavior, industrial sociology —have now yielded a considerable literature, and have provided the basis for advisory services to management by a growing number of consultants.

How the Book Was Written

Given the importance of organizational problems in the universities, why should not more sociological studies be made of them? This was the question that some of us in the Organizational Research Group at the University of North Carolina in 1953 and 1954 began to ask ourselves.

Stephens and Taylor were among the graduate fellows of the Group, and Demerath was one of its co-directors. Like many other professors' products, this book is based in large part on the researches of former students. Part II, "The Presidency: Power at the Top," and part of Chapter 12 come out of Stephens' doctoral dissertation; and Part IV, "The Academic Departments: Power and Reputation," is based upon Taylor's dissertation.[4] Part III, "Administrative Style and Its Effects," comes from a study by Demerath assisted by Taylor.

The factual studies use the same general frame of reference: the university seen as a managed organization wherein the phenomena of power and positions are emphasized. This approach and the work of others who have employed it are the subjects of Chapter 2. Here, attention is directed to the plan of the book.

[4] Richard W. Stephens, *The Academic Administrator: The Role of the University President* (University of North Carolina, Ph.D. dissertation, 1956); R. Robb Taylor, *The American University as a Behavioral System: Power Hierarchies in Selected Academic Departments* (University of North Carolina, Ph.D. dissertation, 1958, also available from University Microfilms, Ann Arbor, Michigan).

We have tried to write for a variety of people concerned with the American university—trustees, administrators, faculty, and friends of higher education. We have tried, also, to write for sociologists and for teachers of administration, though the book is neither a textbook nor a technical monograph. Accordingly, sociological jargon has been reduced to the minimum, and certain statistical and methodological details have been put in an appendix. Thus, we have sought to present our pictures of major American universities with as little clutter for the general reader as possible.

Within the frame of the university seen as a managed organization, the administrative-professional relationship looms large and central. This relationship is viewed first at "the top," in Part II, where the presidents of forty-five major universities between 1930 and 1955 are seen in relation to faculty and trustees, to administrative staff and various publics. Then, in Part III, the influence of the chief executive and his principal deans on faculty behavior and sentiments is observed in a single major university. Finally, Part IV deals with power, esteem, and faculty attitudes in thirty departments of five major universities.

We refer to "major universities." What does this mean? By definition, for present purposes, a major university is one which in 1953–54 met four criteria:

1. Combined a liberal-arts program with a full range of graduate education, including at least five separate schools or colleges (e.g., law, medicine, theology, engineering, education, pharmacy, dentistry, forestry, journalism).

2. Maintained a staff of administrative officials of over fifty, not including their subordinate assistants and clerks (e.g., vice-presidents, provost, business manager, directors, deans).

3. Operated with an annual budget of not less than $10 million.

4. Catered to a student clientele of not less than 5,000.

Among the more than 1,800 accredited colleges and universities in the United States in 1953–54, Stephens found forty-two

TABLE 1-1

Major American Universities of Reference

"Private" (22)	"Public" (23)
Boston University	University of Alabama
° University of Chicago	University of California
Columbia University	University of Georgia
° Cornell University	University of Illinois
Duke University	° Indiana University
Harvard University	University of Iowa
Johns Hopkins University	University of Kansas
Massachusetts Institute of Technology	Louisiana State University
	University of Michigan
New York University	University of Minnesota
° Northwestern University	University of Missouri
° University of Pennsylvania	University of Nebraska
University of Pittsburgh	University of North Carolina
Princeton University	Ohio State University
University of Rochester	University of Oklahoma
University of Southern California	University of Oregon
	Pennsylvania State University
Southern Methodist University	Rutgers University (State University of New Jersey)
Stanford University	University of Texas
Syracuse University	University of Tennessee
Tulane University	University of Virginia
Washington University of St. Louis	University of Washington
	University of Wisconsin
Western Reserve University	
Yale University	

institutions with these specifications.[5] Of these, twenty-two were publicly controlled and supported and twenty were privately controlled and supported. Three other universities (University of Virginia, Duke, and Princeton) were also in-

[5] Three universities—Wayne, Catholic, and St. Louis—had been omitted, because their administrative structures deviated somewhat from those of the rest. Wayne University then was a municipally controlled and supported university, and the other two are operated and supported by the Roman Catholic Church.

cluded, having met all the above criteria except size of student body.[6]

The forty-five universities whose presidencies are studied and some of whose departments are sampled in this book are listed in Table 1-1, the asterisk denoting the latter. The study of succession was made only at the University of North Carolina (Chapel Hill).

Preview

The second chapter, like this one, is an "introduction." Its purpose is to give a background and context for the study of academic administration in the United States. The evolution of the university is outlined, starting in the eleventh and twelfth centuries in Europe. Certain administrative similarities between present-day European and American universities are described. The mixture—it is *not* compound—of two different social forms, bureaucracy and collegium, which characterizes the American university today is explored briefly in anticipation of subsequent chapters. Finally, research by others is summarized.

"The Presidency: Power at the Top" (Part II) is based on a piece of detective work in a body of largely qualitative materials pertaining to the presidencies of the forty-five major universities listed above. Here we have sought to preserve and project the nature of Stephens' research monograph—highly personal, sometimes literary, frequently humorous. The scattered and disparate reports, reminiscences, and anecdotes by and about presidents and their problems were converted to evidence by the method of "content analysis," and interpreted

[6] The survey of universities was based on the current course catalogues published by the institutions and the following statistical publications: United States Office of Education, *Statistics of Higher Education: Receipts, Expenditures, and Property* (Washington: U.S. Government Printing Office, 1953–54); and Mary Irvin, *American Colleges and Universities* (Washington: American Council on Education, 1952).

by means of three principal sociological concepts—office, role, and relationship. The evidence that illuminates the roles of the presidency are what the presidents (and other members of the organization) say they do and should do, and what they say about their sentiments in regard to these roles. A major finding is that the presidency characteristically entails five major organizational roles: Money Man, Administrator, Father Figure, Public-Relations Man, and Educator to the Public. "The job inside" the university comprises the first three roles, and "the job outside," the last two. The second principal finding is that these roles and expectations are quite inconsistent and, thus, evoke a variety of adjustment mechanisms, some of which can hardly be classed as rational administration. The role conflicts and adjustments are seen as important factors in the hiatus between president and faculty. That Stephens' analysis is less impressionistic than it may seem will become evident to those who read the methodological account in Appendix A.

"Administrative Style and Its Effects" (Part III) is based on the study of a succession in top administrative personnel and a change in the manner of academic management over a period of four years at the University of North Carolina (Chapel Hill). Faculty behavior and sentiments with reference to university administration and government were measured first in 1956 by a questionnaire sponsored by the Faculty Council and sent to all full-time members of the faculty. The same questionnaire was again administered, under similar auspices, in 1960—four years after a new chancellor, dean of the faculty, chairman of the faculty, dean of the graduate school, dean of the college, and business manager had been appointed. The principal idea tested was that change of administrative style produces change in the participation, the views, and the sentiments of the organization's members. More particularly, the experiment—termed "quasi" because the investigators did not control the conditions but only exploited the history of an institution—was designed to explore the effects of a "colleague" administration, referred to elsewhere as the "Neo-Scientific Management Model."[7]

"The Academic Departments: Power and Reputation" (Part IV) deals with administrator-faculty and inter-colleague relations within and between academic departments, the primary organizational "cells" of the university. Chapter 9 describes the organization of academic departments, in the light of Taylor's survey of thirty departments, sampled at Chicago, Cornell, Indiana, Northwestern, and Pennsylvania. There is consideration of certain university-wide problems of administration that are rooted in the structures of the academic departments. Chapters 10 and 11 deal with five variables of importance in department behavior: (1) *power* of individual department members, as rated by their colleagues, to influence departmental decisions in fourteen areas of policy-making, such as appointments, budget, promotions, allocation of courses, and recruitment of students; (2) *esteem* or the contribution made by the individual to the intellectual climate of the department, also a matter of colleagues' ratings; (3) *correlation of hierarchies* of power and esteem; (4) the individual's *satisfaction* with nine aspects of his own professional and personal life, including, for example, salary, requisites for good teaching, and social relations with department colleagues; and (5) national *reputation* of the departments, also a rating by members.

The department chairmen were clearly the most powerful people in the thirty departments, though they were not always held in the highest esteem for their contributions to intellectual climates. The departments appeared to be less unitary or monomorphic in power structure than "classic" bureauc-

[7] Nicholas J. Demerath, "Social Behavior, Policy Making, and the Business Enterprise," in M. M. Hargrove, I. H. Harrison, and E. L. Swearingen (eds.), *Business Policy Cases: With Behavioral Science Implications* (Homewood, Ill.: Richard D. Irwin, Inc., 1963).

racies, but hardly the "communities of equals" that academic departments are sometimes said to be. Here, as in business and government, the performance and the satisfactions of personnel were significantly associated; although which was cause and which effect is anybody's guess. Some of the factors of satisfaction are administratively manipulatable. Since the American university now faces a "seller's market" in faculty recruitment, the findings may be especially interesting to academic administrators and talent scouts who would entice academicians.

In the last chapter, "The Case for Collegialized Management," we have sought to assemble the book's principal findings and to explore something of their significance. As the book was written, so was the final chapter: implications have been drawn, significance considered, with both administrators and administrative scientists in mind; not to mention the friends of the university now in jeopardy.

2

The University as a Managed Organization

SINCE OUR VIEW of the university is that of a managed organization, it will be well to explain what we have in mind and to see what there is to the idea substantively. A brief historical summary is followed by a review of prior research, with special reference to the dual structures of power: bureaucratic and collegial. These two sources and systems of power create that ubiquitous tension within universities which is at once the principal problem in the administration of professionals and of the book.

Formal organizations called universities gradually developed during the eleventh and twelfth centuries, beginning in 1158 with the famous University of Bologna, and in 1200 the even more renowned "Mother of Universities," Paris. Previously, smiths, cobblers, armorers, and other craftsmen had associated as "universities" for mutual protection against political oppressions, but it was not until this time that masters and scholars banded together for learning. From Paris migrated the scholars who founded Oxford; from Oxford the founders of Cambridge, and most of the later French and Spanish institutions. These were followed by the Universities of Prague, Heidelberg, Vienna, Cologne, Copenhagen, and Lisbon—all admitted imitators of the University of Paris.[1] Institutions of higher education in the United States, springing as they do from the original Harvard College, are indirectly descended from Cambridge, from whose Emmanuel College came Harvard's founding fathers.

Until the founding of Johns Hopkins in 1876, there were no universities in the United States in the European sense. Beginning with Harvard in 1636, all institutions of higher learning founded before the Civil War were colleges of "liberal arts." Like Harvard, they were founded by and for theologians, and to prepare leaders in the learned professions and in civil affairs. Patterned after the liberal-arts colleges of Cambridge or Oxford, the early American college provided a curriculum based on grammar, logic, rhetoric, mathematics, astronomy, and theology. Students bound for professions other than the ministry supplemented these courses with apprenticeships to lawyers or doctors.[2]

Originally, boards of trustees, regents, or overseers were appointed by the founders to act as guardians of orthodoxy, and as aides to the professors in getting support for their institutions. Boards were mainly comprised of clergymen and prominent local merchants and lawyers. Invariably, a minister was elected by the board to serve as president of the college and to be responsible for maintaining discipline and for inculcating Reformation-Protestant ethics. Usually, the president was the first teacher among the faculty. Often he was

---

[1] K. A. Sarafian, "The Rise of Universities during the Middle Ages," *Education*, XLVII (March 1937), 387–92; C. H. Haskins, *The Rise of Universities* (New York: Knopf and Co., 1916), p. 20.

[2] W. Rudy, "The Revolution in American Higher Education, 1865–1900," *Harvard Educational Review*, XXIV (summer 1951), 44.

about the only one. It was not uncommon for the president to teach every course in the catalogue and still continue an active preaching career. In 1802 the president of Princeton, by board edict, was required to preside at faculty meetings and to execute their decisions; to preside at commencement and other ceremonies; to arrange and lead morning and evening prayers and Sunday worship; to lecture on the evidences of Christianity and on any other subjects he might choose; and, finally, to attend to the general superintendence of the college and to promote its interest and reputation at every opportunity. As late as 1850 this regulation was the same, word for word.[3]

Before the Civil War the college faculty, characteristically, was small and its members educated in a uniform way. Administrative matters were rarely complex, and were usually disposed of in round-table discussions between the president and the faculty. Except for librarians, employed occasionally by the more affluent institutions, the president was the only administrative officer. He was generally portrayed in the literature of the period as venerable and benign; as a paternal figure with noble brow and antiquarian tastes; as a sage bellwether of a little flock of scholars, all of them browsing pretty much at will.[4]

Today's American university is said to have emerged from the desire of mid-nineteenth-century educators to combine three conceptions of an institution of higher learning: (1) the British concept of a college for the making of educated gentlemen, which characterized American institutions before 1876; (2) the German concept of a graduate university pursuing knowledge for its own sake, which was introduced with the founding of Johns Hopkins and was gradually accepted by the larger privately controlled colleges of the time; and (3) the

[3] G. P. Schmidt, *The Old Time College President* (New York: Columbia University Press, 1930), p. 54.

[4] *New Republic*, "The Decline of College Presidents," IV (September 4, 1915), 203.

American concept of a university supported by the people and justifying itself by serving their needs, the idea that is associated especially with the great state universities.[5]

As a fourth concept, or perhaps a variant of the third, the contemporary American university is also regarded as an integral part of an advanced technological society. That is, it is seen as a source of socio-economic momentum and of scientifically trained manpower. And this is the case not only in the United States but also in the U.S.S.R. and in Western Europe. A. H. Halsey has traced this contemporary concept and function to the industrial applications of science in the nineteenth century, and to the search for high productivity (and the arms race) during and after World War II.

Both as research organizations and as training establishments, the institutions of higher education in this period have been drawn more closely into the economy either directly or through the state. The exchange of ideas, people, and contracts between university departments and research institutes and their counterparts in private industry and government agencies is such as to merge their organizations and to assimilate the life styles of their staff.[6]

Whatever else this increased exchange with the economy and state may entail, it has probably accentuated bureaucratization and thus heightened the tension between collegial and bureaucratic elements in the universities of Europe as well as of the United States. Correspondingly, this trend seems to have highlighted the problems of administering professionals.

Lest the reader think the problem of "Power, Presidents, and Professors" is peculiar to the United States, brief notice of the situation in some European countries will be in order. There is little doubt that the European professor participates more in university government than does his American counterpart. The governing board of laymen as such does not

[5] Rudy, *op. cit.*, p. 43.

[6] "The Changing Functions of Universities in Advanced Industrial Societies," *Harvard Educational Review*, 30 (spring 1960), 123.

exist in Europe. And although the ministries of education in most European countries have wielded considerable influence in internal university affairs, the officials have usually been academicians.

Yet, all of this is rather deceptive. It should be noted that faculty participation in Europe is generally restricted to *full* professors: those of lesser rank have much less voice there than in the United States. They have very little to say even in their own departments, where all authority is vested in department chairmen. Moreover, in response to public demand for closer university-society relationships and with the increasing complexity of university operations, particularly in matters of finance and the administration of plant facilities, professorial power seems to be diminishing. In Germany, the Minister of Education is a political appointee. His advisory council, over half of whose members were formerly elected by university faculties, is now made up of professional and business people whom he appoints. The rectors are being elected for terms longer than one year, and their responsibilities have been gradually extended. In France, universities now include local lay officials on their advisory councils.[7]

In Britain, the central government has long provided a substantial portion of the financial resources of English universities. Since 1946 these appropriations have increased to a point where as much as eighty per cent of university resources are government funds. Increasingly, university officials seem to believe that government control of these funds is becoming more and more restrictive and detailed. Similarly, although the universities are formally independent of the rest of the educational system, the more they become involved in extramural or

[7] E. A. Fitzpatrick, "His Magnificence: The Rector in the German University," *School and Society*, LXXV (May 1952), 164; and H. K. Newburn, "The Organization and Administration of Universities in France, Italy, and Great Britain," *Educational Record*, XXXIV (July 1953), 261–6.

other programs of local or state interest, the more influence is brought to bear on educational affairs, which is difficult to disregard. Power relations between faculties and administrators in more countries might be cited as evidence of the extensiveness of the problem that concerns us here. To do so, however, would be to digress further from our main subject.

The American University Today: Bureaucracy and Collegium

The time when faculty and students were accountable only to themselves and to the ultimate civil or religious authority has passed. Centralized administrations with full-time officials have supplanted the bona fide faculty members chosen by colleagues to represent their institution before the public, and to co-ordinate faculty activities. The members of governing boards are rarely scholars, and the professional administrator —whatever his familiarity with payrolls—may never have met a class or written a book. In the first chapter we referred to the university as a most peculiar kind of organization whose historic mission—the nurture of mind and spirit—is in jeopardy. Here, attention is directed to the root problem and phenomenon: the dual structures of power, bureaucratic and collegial, or, as they are also termed, executive and professional.

As liberal-arts colleges became universities—often a matter initially of imposing a graduate school or adding a single professional curriculum—academic administration became specialized, differentiated, and bureaucratic. And as universities grew in number of specialty departments and other units— students and faculty, service clienteles and claimants, income sources and amounts—so have their administrations tended to become increasingly specialized, differentiated, and bureaucratic. Moreover, the growth of our universities has been very rapid. For example, total income, always related to administrative functions, has doubled every ten years since 1876; and since 1930 total income has more than quadrupled.

The appearance of new positions gives evidence of the trend. In 1887 the first registrar was employed in a university; in 1889 the first vice-president; in 1891 the first dean of faculties; and in 1906 the first business manager. Appropriate deans, secretaries, directors, and provosts followed. Then, in the 1950's, came the management consultants seeking fees and "self-surveys"; universities had become big enterprises and were now aware of it. Changes were effected in academic and faculty organization. Departments were given standardized definitions and put into divisions by subject matter. Instructional activities, student-personnel activities, research work, fund-raising, alumni activities, and public relations were separated, defined officially, and placed under the direction of responsible officers.

More visible than the collegial structure is the university as prescribed by law and regulation: this structure can be charted and labeled, given signs and symbols. This is the blueprint for bureaucracy, the official structure of the modern university. As with most complex managed organizations, the university's bureaucratic structure reveals a three-dimensional pyramidal pattern. From the board and the president at the apex, lines of communication extend downward through levels of organization: deans, directors, department chairmen, professors, and students. Horizontally, on each level range coordinating agencies: the major colleges or schools, the divisions (e.g., arts and sciences, physical sciences), the various service units (e.g., adult education, extension service), the several departments within each division or school, and the various courses within each department. Although chains of command, in which superiors give orders to subordinates, are usually confined to the service departments (accounting, buildings and grounds, etc.), specific and formal responsibilities are assigned or delegated officials on all levels, the ultimate responsibility for general policy residing in the external governing board. This, in general, is the university in its official dimension, the university of the administrators. But this official structure is only a part of the action organization of people behaving. There is also the collegium.

The collegial structure of the university is juxtaposed and often opposed to the official form. As any one-time officer learns, especially when he forsakes "the power and glory" of a chairmanship or deanship to be a pure professor again, laymen find his action exceedingly strange. They mistakenly think administrators give orders to full professors, who give orders to associate professors, and so on "down" through the assistant professors and instructors. Second, laymen are often unaware of the academician's self-image as a professional whose work is the *sine qua non* in the university's primary tasks: the advancement, the preservation, and the transmission of knowledge. In academic work, the university is not unlike a symphony orchestra. Although the conductor may be an adamant "director," the first-chairs do not transmit orders by chains of command to the second-chairs, the third-chairs, etc., for execution. In the collegial structure, a traditional and even formal status hierarchy may exist that superficially resembles the status hierarchy of the government agency or industry, but these hierarchies do not work in the same way. Hence the importance of distinguishing the dual structures, bureaucratic and collegial, that give form to the university and its educational processes.

The collegial structure can best be seen in terms of its personnel, the faculty, who are the "key operatives" in the university. In relation to them, other personnel of the university provide supportive services. Non-faculty personnel are there to make it possible for the faculty and the students to discharge their responsibilities. The students are a major

23

clientele: they are members of the larger society who receive the benefits of the faculty's activities directly. Students are also a principal "raw material" of the university: they enter the university in one state of knowledge and viewpoint and, it is hoped, leave it in another. It is the faculty, theoretically, who are mainly responsible for the transformation.

Although the faculty member does most of the teaching and research in the university, he does other things, too. It is seldom that presidents, vice-presidents, or deans engage in teaching or research, but it is not uncommon for professors to participate in administration. Faculty members serve as department chairmen, as part-time deans, and as members and chairmen of committees (some extremely powerful and university-wide), and yet remain "primarily" scholars and teachers. In these capacities, they represent their colleague constituencies before other faculty and with the top administration—and perhaps before the general public. They are commonly expected to co-ordinate the activities of their colleagues and their students, and in doing so they plan, make policy, and carry out decisions. Thus, the professor acts both in an administrative capacity and in an operative one, the former taking him away from the strict specialization characteristic of the classic bureaucracy.

As Caplow has noted, there exists in the modern university a faculty-member continuum. At one end is complete specialization in teaching and research, and at the other end is the total abandonment of these activities. The professor who steadfastly refuses to accept any obligations—even membership on department committees—that would interfere with his teaching or research activities is "poles apart" from the non-teaching dean who devotes his time and effort exclusively to administration.[8]

[8] Theodore Caplow and Reece J. McGee, *The Academic Marketplace* (New York: Basic Books, 1958).

The non-teaching dean is a common target for disgruntled students or faculty members, as is illustrated by the aphorisms about the dean "too smart to be a college president but not smart enough to be a professor" and the assistant dean who is "a mouse training to be a rat." Frequently the non-teaching dean's career began as a vestige of the early American and European community of scholars. He carried on his teaching and research activities. Later, his administrative task was enlarged to include increasingly important posts on campus committees, and then he became so overburdened that time for teaching and research disappeared. His academic career ends in a central or top administrative office. He no longer sets foot in a classroom, a library, or a laboratory, though his name continues to be listed in the university catalogue as a faculty member.

Between the poles of the pure specialist with no time for his academic community, and the full-time administrator with no time for academics, are the participants in the collegial structure of the university. We refer to the committee men whose committees count in policy matters, and to the administrators who remain active, though restricted, teachers and scholars. It is they who, in behalf of their constituencies, act to modify, tame, and curb the powers of the full-time administrators which derive from the corporate authority of the institution, as interpreted by board and president. This they do in several ways, as the great German sociologist Max Weber observed. (1) They may occupy positions whose duties call for review, delay, or veto. (2) The full-time administrator's intended action may first have to be cleared by consultation and vote in a body of advisors. (3) There may be a number of full-time administrators whose authority is the same, whose jurisdictions are unclear, and who hold veto power over one another. (4) Finally, as illustrated by the position of the British prime minister in his cabinet, the official may be *primus inter pares,* his position dependent upon the continued support of his cabinet colleagues, who can resign.

As Weber also observed, members of a collegial body often gain the upper hand with the chief because, should he not accede to their recommendations, he may be made to suffer the consequences for his independence of action. As a strategy, members of the collegium may create a division of labor and specialization of functions such that each person becomes a technical expert more knowledgeable in his own area than any of his colleagues, including the chief. Knowledge being power, the members of the collegium thereby gain ascendancy.

Weber noted certain weaknesses in the collegial form of organization, namely: (1) obstacles are placed in the way of rapid and precise decisions; (2) consistency and co-ordination of policies and activities are affected negatively; (3) the responsibilities of office holders are imprecise; and (4) discipline within the group is usually impaired. These characteristics, Weber thought, are commonly forces making for the transformation of collegia into bureaucracies. They are surely forces for tension in the American university—tensions that may call forth highly original administrative responses and educational achievements, as James Perkins has noted.[9] On the other hand, they may also produce the kind of institutional paralysis and stalemate observed by Lazarsfeld, as quoted in Chapter 1.

Correlates of the Bureaucratic and Collegial Mixture

So much for description of the bureaucratic and collegial dimensions of the university. What has been said by way of

[9] James Perkins, "Moral Judgment and Academic Structures," in Harlan Cleveland and Harold Lasswell (eds.), *Ethics and Bigness* (New York: Harper & Bros., 1962).

explanation or analysis? Few social scientists have published on the problem, and some of these only incidentally. Almost twenty-five years ago, in a study of thirty major universities, Logan Wilson noted the impact of bureaucratization, and considered—especially in a chapter titled "The Professor Administrant—various aspects of the administration-faculty relationship, though chiefly as experienced by the professor.[10] Before Wilson there had been Thorstein Veblen (*The Higher Learning in America*, 1915), but, since Wilson, there have been few efforts to deal with the executive-professional problem, even indirectly,[11] although some attempts have been made to study administrative-teacher relations systematically in secondary education.[12]

The mixture of bureaucratic and collegial elements which structures the university as a managed organization gives rise to three questions: What are the outcomes? Is the mixture necessary? If it is necessary, what is the optimum combination of bureaucracy and collegium?

As to the outcomes or correlates of the dual structures, numerous authors, writing from personal experience, have observed differences and tension between administrators and academicians. Woodrow Wilson, who moved from Princeton to the White House, referred to "the perennial misunderstanding" between men who write and men who act. He saw it in the daily encounters between administrators and faculty. A one-time dean observed that faculty members commonly regard administrators as lowly sub-professionals whose proper

[10] Logan Wilson, *The Academic Man* (New York: Oxford University Press, 1942).

[11] One exception should be noted: Charles H. Page, "Bureaucracy in Higher Education," *Journal of General Education*, 11 (January 1951), 91–100.

[12] A good bibliography and evaluation of this and other aspects of sociological research, in elementary as well as in secondary education, is Orville Brim, *Sociology and the Field of Education* (New York: Russell Sage Foundation, 1958).

job is not to manage the university but to serve the faculty in their academic pursuits. Correspondingly, the faculty oppose hierarchy and favor "horizontal administration in the extreme."[13] Many conflicts in the university are thought to stem from basic differences over hierarchical (i.e., bureaucratic) relationships; and it behooves the administrator who would make changes in policy to avoid casting scholars as subordinates.[14]

Such random observations as these are verified in the more systematic study of several institutions by the sociologists Caplow and McGee. They found a high incidence of conflict, a ". . . widespread and passionate dissatisfaction of professors with the workings of academic government."[15] That the relative strengths of the parties to the conflict in any university may be of broader significance has been suggested, though not tested.

It may even be argued that one of the reliable indicators of the quality of a university is how "strong" the faculty is vis-à-vis the administration. A weak administration does not make an outstanding faculty, but an outstanding faculty may demand a weak administration.[16]

Other correlates more germane to the book's problem than the general tension between administrators and professors are the stuctures of power and decision-making under conditions of mixed bureaucracy and collegium. Storm and Finkle, public-administration specialists, have analyzed succinctly and well the power that derives from the fact that academicians

[13] Harlan Cleveland, "The Dean's Dilemma: Leadership of Equals," *Public Administration Review,* XX, 1 (winter 1960), 23.

[14] John D. Millett, *The Academic Community: An Essay on Organization* (New York: McGraw-Hill, 1962), pp. 179, 232–3.

[15] *The Academic Marketplace,* p. 208.

[16] William B. Storm and Jason Finkle, *American Professionals in Technical Assistance: A Preliminary Report* (Los Angeles: School of Public Administration, University of Southern California, 1965), p. 16.

are specialists and professionals. The paragraphs following mainly paraphrase their account.[17]

Bureaucratic ladders of ability-rank-authority, supposedly parallel, are difficult, if not impossible, to establish in a university faculty because of the collegial organization and the dual system of ranking. Academic rank is conferred by the university, but prestige in the discipline is awarded by outsiders, the latter being a matter of judgment by one's academic peers and not subject to the local institution's control. Most academic professionals value disciplinary prestige and its acknowledged expertise more highly than academic rank. And although university officials often try to adjust rank to prestige by considering the evaluations of "outsiders" when faculty members are to be appointed or promoted, any given rank will include men of varying prestige. Power, therefore, cannot be tied to specific positions in the form of authority, for, as Cleveland, Caplow, and McGee point out, such an allocation of authority would establish relationships of subordination and inequality which are inconsistent with the social facts of collegium.[18]

Though faculty members may lack authority of office, they possess influence. This influence or potential influence of an individual faculty member seems mainly a matter of his functional proximity to the university's goals, his length of tenure, his prestige, and, related to these, his known ability to move elsewhere on short notice. Thus, as Cleveland observed, the scholar's career depends less on his position within the authority structure of his own institution than on his repute as a specialist. The tenured professor who can move elsewhere has influence if he cares to exercise it, and his influence amounts to a kind of veto power over administrative autocracy.

[17] *Ibid.*, pp. 10–13.
[18] Cleveland, *op. cit.*; Caplow and McGee, *op. cit.*

This pattern of power and influence is reflected in the decision-making process in the university. Princeton's former president Dodds, speaking to this point, has observed that an experienced businessman undertaking to work for a university has some radical psychological adjustments to a social system in which the decision-making process is more widely dispersed than in business.[19] Specialization, the freedom of inquiry and communication, the external and disciplinary orientation of participants, and the influence potential of the academic professional all make for the dispersal and decentralization of decision-making.

Faculties make many decisions affecting the basic activities of the university—i.e., curricula, courses, admission of students, faculty appointments, promotions, and student affairs. The academic departments tend to be quite autonomous in the determination of such matters. Less responsibility is focused in the chief executive and the governing board than is the case in other enterprises. Although Fesler has noted that specialism and individuality of professors reduce their effectiveness as collective decision-makers, the professors nevertheless have felt the need for a policy voice in order to protect freedom of inquiry and teaching, and the recognition of professional competence, and they have insisted on having such a voice.[20]

Necessity of Mixed Organization

Turning to the second question posed by the mixture of bureaucratic and collegial elements in university organization, we ask: Is the mixture necessary? To get at this question, one must have an idea of how the combination came about and

[19] Harold W. Dodds, "Some Thoughts on the University Presidency," *Public Administration Review*, XX, 1 (winter 1960), 14–15.
[20] James W. Fesler, "In Analyzing University Administration," *Public Administration Review*, XX, 1 (winter 1960), 59.

what interests it serves. Several authors have described the personal values, attitudes, and expectations of scientists and scholars as a kind of "family of factors" making for bureaucratic-collegial and, more broadly, executive-professional mixtures. For example, Shepard thinks several of the values and expectations of scientists learned in graduate school and laboratory will not be accepted or served in the usual executive structure.

1. Full opportunity to express, review, and debate ideas and facts.

2. Independence of thought, inquiry, and creativity.

3. Respect for the authority of scientific fact and not social power.

4. Freedom to set one's own tasks and objectives, and then to change them.

5. Dictation of "decisions of breadth" by the weight of scientific opinion.

6. Secrecy as anathema to the scientific community.

7. Confidence and trust, and not intrigue, as implicit in scientific method.

8. Personal development through colleague relations at work.

9. The concept of management as alien.

How behavioral, how practiced, these desiderata are may be questioned. Nevertheless, Marcson, in his study of an industrial-research laboratory, finds colleague and executive administration sufficiently differentiated that he sets them apart as separate administrative forms and styles. Blau and Scott, in a useful review of the literature, came to the same distinction but called it "professional" and "bureaucratic." The distinction is especially clear, they think, when one observes professional people *in* a bureaucracy.

It is clear that this type of control structure differs greatly from that employed in bureaucratic organizations. The source of discipline within a bureaucracy is not the colleague group but the hierarchy of authority. Performance is controlled by directives received from one's superiors rather than by self-imposed standards and peer group surveillance, as is the case among professionals.

31

Similar distinctions have also been made by other organizational analysts.[21]

What the academician expects of the university administration and officialdom has been stated by Millet:[22]

The academic professional expects that the system of organization and operation of his university will recognize the importance of the role of the faculty member and will provide him with a status of dignity and consideration.

The college or university scholar does not think of himself as an *employee* of the university, and he resents the suggestion that his relationship to a dean, a vice-president for academic affairs, and a president involves supervisory authority.

The academician is an individual professional practitioner of scholarship. His learning, his ability as a teacher, and his competence in research cannot be ordered by a dean or other official of the college or university. They can be exercised only as the individual is moved by pride in himself and his profession to make the most of them.

Finally, he expects freedom to pursue his profession of scholarship, and he expects the academic community to protect his privilege to instruct students and to advance knowledge without external pressure and without the requirements of social approval.

One sees two professional postures drawn above: first, the academician committed to scholarly and scientific values antithetical to bureaucracy; second, the academician expecting officials to facilitate his work as a free professional person, while taking care not to order him about as though he were an employee. Both perspectives neglect the university as an institution or organization, though they do not deny the neces-

[21] Herbert Shepard, in A. H. Rubinstein and C. J. Haberstroh (eds.), *Some Theories of Organization* (Homewood, Ill.: The Dorsey Press and Richard D. Irwin, Inc., 1960); Simon Marcson, *The Scientist in American Industry* (Princeton, N.J.: Princeton University, Industrial Relations Section, 1960), pp. 121–41; Peter M. Blau and W. Richard Scott, *Formal Organizations* (San Francisco: Chandler, 1962), p. 63. Distinctions by others are noted in N. J. Demerath, "Social Behavior, Policy Making, and the Business Enterprise," *op. cit.* (Chapter 1).

[22] *The Academic Community,* pp. 101–03.

sity of *some* bureaucratic administration. The problem of bureaucratic adaptation to the attitudes and expectations of academic professionals is not treated.

Storm and Finkle, however, make the adaptation idea central to their account. Following Corson,[23] they state that the modern university organization represents an adaptation, not only to academic tradition, but to general goals and functions (best left open-ended and general for scholarly purposes, i.e., preservation, transmission, advancement of knowledge). Goal accomplishment depends on individual scholars free to investigate and communicate. Therefore, the scholars must be insulated or protected from negative pressures outside the university, and from absolute authority within it. Further, these goals, functions, and preconditions are best served by flat rather than hierarchical relations of power and interpersonal contact.[24]

The extreme specialization of academicians presents another condition to which the university organization must adapt. With specialization goes the academic man's sense of individualism and autonomy. Committed to the authority of knowledge, the academician is disinclined to accept bureaucratic direction and control. And the administrator, for his part, cannot hope to make competent decisions across a wide range of problems and specialty areas, even though he may be qualified in one specialty. Should he forget this and presume to act otherwise, groups and associations of specialists—socialized from graduate-school days to put their disciplines and academic values first—stand ready to correct the errant officials.[25]

Of course, not all academicians are equally committed to collegial values; nor are all administrators alike in their com-

[23] John J. Corson, *The Governance of College and Universities* (New York: McGraw-Hill, 1960), pp. 4–5.
[24] Storm and Finkle, *op. cit.*, pp. 6–7.
[25] *Ibid.*, pp. 8–9.

33

mitments either to bureaucratic principles or to particular institutions. In both camps one may expect to find "cosmopolitans" and "locals," their numbers and ratios varying considerably as between universities, it would seem, although the few studies reported have dealt with faculty members and have not compared institutions. Caplow and McGee, studying employment practices in their sample of American universities, concluded:

Today, a scholar's orientation to his institution is apt to disorient him to his discipline and to affect his professional prestige unfavorably. Conversely, an orientation to his discipline will disorient him to his institution, which he will regard as a temporary shelter where he can pursue his career as a member of the discipline.[26]

Gouldner, studying a small Midwestern college, found that high professional commitments (cosmopolitanism) went with low loyalty to the college.[27] Reviewing these and other studies, some from non-academic settings, in the light of their own research in a public-welfare agency, Blau and Scott concluded:

. . . a commitment to professional skills will be associated with low organizational loyalty *only* if professional *opportunities* [italics ours] are more limited in the organization under consideration than in others with which it competes for manpower.[28]

From the analysis above, one concludes that the collegial dimension of university organization is necessary if these institutions are to continue to discharge their historic, primary functions. What about the executive or bureaucratic dimension? Its necessity is dictated by the very size, complexity, and accountability of universities in modern bureaucratized societies. Also the executive imperative for universities is indi-

[26] *The Academic Marketplace*, p. 85.

[27] Alvin W. Gouldner, "Cosmopolitans and Locals," *Administrative Science Quarterly*, 2 (1957–58), 281–306, 44–480.

[28] *Formal Organizations*, p. 71.

cated by the studies of organization versus professional commitment just referred to above. In connection with the organization's requirements, students of business and government, moreover, have explicated the role of the executive generalist in a context of line and staff reminiscent of the academic situation. Roethlisberger, for example, has pointed to the tendency of the staff specialist to interpret and evaluate organizational objectives in terms of his own specialty, because he is hired to accomplish a particular task. The administrator, Roethlisberger notes, has the more general responsibility of maintaining efficiency through co-ordination and collaboration. Therefore, he is more likely to see the organization as a whole and to analyze accomplishment in quite different terms.[29] In similar vein, Kenneth Burke referred to the specialist as being "fitted by an unfit fitness," and Harold Laski wrote of the "trained incapacity" of the technical specialist—his failure to see things in their entirety, his aversion to new ideas, his suspicion of non-specialist ideas, and so forth.[30] Sociologists Moore and Tumin discuss the possibility of the specialist's using his special knowledge as a weapon for preserving his own status without regard to the organization as such.[31]

Although line and staff situations in business and government may remind us of universities, they are by no means the same. In universities it is the members of the learned professions who are the line workers. And it is they, the professionals, who prefer to view the bureaucratic officials as staff. The latter, however, can scarcely share the academicians' view, given the official university and its structures under law

[29] Fritz J. Roethlisberger, *Management and Morale* (Cambridge: Harvard University Press, 1944), p. 151.

[30] "The Limitations of the Expert," *Harper's,* CLXII (December 1930), 102–06.

[31] Wilbert E. Moore and Melvin M. Tumin, "Some Social Functions of Ignorance," *American Sociological Review,* XIV (December 1948), 789.

and charter. In any case, mixture of the bureaucratic and collegial is necessary.

Optimum Mixture

Bernard Barber has considered our third question: Given the necessity of a mixed organization, what is the optimum mixture? He describes three modes of accommodation which may reduce "the inherent strain between professional roles and organizational necessities": (1) to segregate the professionals from the administrators and line operatives (e.g., corporations create special departments for their lawyers or medical personnel); (2) to establish different rewards and incentives that appeal to professionals (e.g., opportunities to publish, to take part in professional meetings, to advance in salary and prestige by strictly professional achievement); and (3) "to create differentiated authority structures."[32]

Barber's third mechanism seems to be the one most applicable to the university power problem, as we have delineated it here. His analysis merits quoting:

. . . organizations that use professionals can also usually create a specialized type of authority which is an accommodation between the organization's need for the pattern of superordinate control and the professional's need for the colleague control pattern of authority. The key role in this accommodative and specialized authority structure is played by the "professional-administrator." The occupant of this role must be a professional who can judge and direct another professional but (and!) who can also exercise superordinate control when necessary. It is the function of the professional-administrator to grant as much autonomy as possible in the choice and evaluation of professional work, while providing over-all direction and co-ordination with the primary goals of the organization . . . Where many professionals are employed, there

[32] "Some Problems in the Sociology of the Professions," *Daedalus*, XC, 4 (fall 1963) 680–2. See also William Kornhauser, *Scientists in Industry: Conflict and Accommodation* (Berkeley: University of California Press, 1962).

may be a hierarchy of professional-administrators. The higher the administrator's position in this hierarchy, the more his concern is with the problems of co-ordination for the whole organization in which the professionals are employed.[33]

To approach the optimal authority structure in any university—not to mention the optimal power structure which, by definition, comprises *both* authority and influence—is very difficult. It is hard to find enough administrators (Wilson's term "professor-administrant" seems to be what Barber means, not just any professional administrator) with the right combination of abilities. Moreover, the roles are subject to pressures from both camps. More empirical work on these and related questions is needed as a basis for guided change and creative innovating.

With what seems to be a growing concern as to how best to develop and utilize professionals in industry and government, in health and welfare, in research laboratories, as well as in the universities, it is likely that the administration of professionals will attract more students and more innovators. Our studies, we hope, will make some contribution, however modest, to this development.

[33] *Ibid.*, p. 681.

PART II

The Presidency:
Power at the Top

3

Trustees and the
Selection of Presidents

IN THE more bureaucratic dimension of university organization, the presidency is the pivotal office: it is comparatively
well defined in its legal formalities, is clearly top-rung on the
ladders of authority and status, and is the university's principal
link with the ultimate powers and resources of the larger
society. In its collegial dimension, also, university organization
is by no means immune to the forces of the presidency, no
matter how strong and independent the faculty. Part creature
and part creator of the organization in which he works, the
university president, like other chief executives, is expected
to maintain the organizational structure and to give leadership
to the making of general policy decisions. Moreover, he is
expected to express organizational objectives in terms of
values intended to guide decisions at lower levels of the organization.

The present chapter is devoted mainly to the process by
which presidents are selected, and the boards of trustees who

do the choosing. It is the board of trustees that holds the prime legal power in university administration. The other power source lies in the faculty and in various veto groups, within and outside the university. Historically, the collegiate board of trustees represented the interests of a laity in educational affairs. They were held responsible, by statute or custom, for the general oversight and legislative direction necessary to ensure the proper execution of a trust. They were the custodians of the institution's income, expenditure, and property, to use or dispose of as they saw fit. They selected the president, hired the teachers, determined admission policies and degree requirements, outlined programs of study, handled faculty promotion and tenure. The early boards relied on the presidents and the faculties for day-to-day educational management, but they rarely considered either as more than their employees, to be selected and dismissed at will. The boards usually comprised prominent local business and professional men, and were more or less representative of those who had established and first maintained the institutions. The usual board had less than fifteen members and was conservative and paternalistic in most respects.

What Trustees Do

Over the years, major changes have occurred in the practices of boards which have produced in the modern university a structure of power and authority that distinguishes it from other types of managed organizations. A fundamental change took place about 1900, when most boards delegated all educational-policy determination to the president and the faculty. The boards retained only legal control over curricula, admission and degree requirements, and faculty recruitment. And this control came to be viewed as a paper right or legal fiction.

Just why this delegation occurred is puzzling. Historically, the boards seemed to guard jealously their rights to develop educational policies and to control educational practices. Especially were they on guard against the penetration of alien "isms." The most likely explanation may be that, with their increased size and differentiation, universities came to have problems too numerous and complex for laymen who met infrequently and who usually had limited contact with academic circles. Moreover, as the composition of boards changed from local community representatives to regional or national financiers and industrialists, so did their predominant concerns change to finance, plant, and budget—for which the members felt themselves best equipped, and which they were least inclined to leave to the academicians.

Although an occasional board is accused of exercising its educational responsibilities unduly by flouting traditions of academic freedom or tenure, a majority seem to see themselves as policy-making or legislative bodies who should keep out of administration. The few boards who, in recent years, have sought to recast faculty-personnel policies on grounds of perceived Communist dangers have chosen to exercise a historic and legal right. Whether or not boards of trustees are now "interfering" in educational matters more often, particularly with regard to the selection of faculty, is debatable. As one writer pointed out, in educational matters boards usually tend to be amiable and honored rubber stamps. When situations are politically charged, however, boards may be sensitive to the press and to pressure groups and may thus react, not by defending the university, but by partaking in a witch hunt until the institution proves itself innocent.

As a legislative agency, the modern board exercises its historic responsibility of setting the general goals and policies of the university. Also, it still aids in the collection of revenue, and is active in the control of all other money matters, including salaries. In the 1930's the comptroller or business manager of the university was often directly responsible to the board for the administration of fiscal policies. Sometimes the business manager served as secretary to the board or was a full member of it. This arrangement has been superseded in most universities by "the *unit* arrangement," in which the president is responsible to the board, and the business manager is subordinate to the president. In both financial and educational matters, boards of trustees now rely more and more on the advice of the president and his staff, particularly in the allocation of funds among the several schools and departments. Indeed, a number of trustees now believe that the principal job of the board is to select the president. By retaining this privilege, the board is able to maintain important control over long-run university operations and policies.

Who the Trustees Are

The number of members on governing boards varies from five to 100, with a median number of nine. The size of a board seems loosely related to the range of interests to which the institution appeals, and to whether it is publicly or privately controlled. In one study of 114 university charters, the privately controlled universities had more board members, on the average, than those publicly controlled. Moreover, the privately controlled institutions tended over time to enlarge, and the publicly controlled to diminish, their memberships. Changes in number were attributed to several factors, including the desire to add alumni, the consolidation of several institutions under one board, efforts to add specific types of individuals, reorganization due to expansion, and movement away from denominational control.

Most trustees desire small boards, usually of not less than seven or more than fifteen members. This attitude is generally shared by presidents, who usually reason that a member of a smaller board feels more responsible for its actions and for the program of the university. Moreover, smaller boards can meet more easily and oftener. One president noted that smaller boards tended less to interfere in administrative affairs, being busier with their own concerns.

Except in those state universities where members are appointed by the governors or elected by the people, boards of trustees do not directly represent any identifiable group of citizens, nor do they represent faculties or students. In most cases, the boards themselves select their new members when terms of office expire or vacancies occur otherwise. Often, members are elected for life, or for whatever period they are willing to serve actively. A few of a board's members may be alumni of the institution, but most new board members are selected because they (1) have money or influence which the universities need, (2) have reputations for getting money, or (3) represent influential groups or constituencies other than alumni. To boards of state universities, it has been suggested, governors are usually under pressure to appoint individuals to whom they owe political favors. Board memberships are sought eagerly, and provide a comparatively simple way of meeting political obligations. Such appointees often value their offices as sources of influence or dispensation, through business contracts, honorary degrees, or student-parent benefits.

The concentration of business leaders and financiers on boards of trustees appears to have increased over the years, and has long been a subject of controversy among educators and among such writers as Thorstein Veblen (*The Higher Learning in America,* 1915) and Ferdinand Lundberg (*America's 60 Families,* 1937). From 1860 to 1930, one survey of boards found that the percentage of businessmen on the boards of thirty leading American universities increased from twenty-seven to fifty-two per cent, whereas the combined percentages from theology, law, medicine, and education dropped from seventy to forty-six—most of the loss occurring among clergymen. In the same period, the combined percentages of lawyers, businessmen, and bankers increased from forty-eight to seventy-three.

45

This change in the composition of the governing board can be attributed largely to the changing character of the academic institution itself. From a small college with modest resources and a localized board that knew all the faculty members and many of the students, the institution has burst forth into a rich corporation with an endowment spread over many investments. Today, trustees are drawn from many parts of the country, and can maintain intimate relationships with no more than a few of their university's staff. In many respects, their function is that of a board of directors whose foremost desire is to keep the plant expanding and under the direction of an effective manager. The rest is up to the president.

The Presidential Office

Boards expect much of presidents. The selection-succession problem is of the utmost gravity. And no wonder. The president is the man on whom the trustees must depend for advice and for the execution of board decisions. Unless there is a close and congenial working relation between the board and the president, frictions can be expected until the president dies, resigns, or is removed. Through the president, the board has the power to influence the outlook, trend, and tenor of the university, and one need only consider the turnover rate of presidents to appreciate the frequency with which this power is exercised. Undoubtedly the selection and appointment of a new president is a momentous event in the life of the university. For most of the trustees, it represents their first and only chance to share in this important function, inasmuch as the term of the president is usually longer than the terms of the majority of his board.

Presidential tenures are thought to be shorter than they actually are. Some have said that the academic president these days lasts only about four years in a given job. However,

W. K. Selden, in a survey of the presidencies of 1,300 colleges and universities that belonged to the National Commission on Accrediting in 1959, found that the current presidents had been in office an average 8.1 years.[1] Since 1900, excluding current and acting presidents, the average was 11.4 years for these institutions. Comparing institutions of different size, those with enrollments of 5,000 and more—the category that includes the "major universities" studied by Stephens—held out a somewhat briefer tenure prospect (10.9 years on the average) than did all but the smallest, those with less than 1,000 (10.4 years). For those with enrollments between 1,000 and 5,000, the average tenure between 1900 and 1959 was the greatest (almost twelve years).[2]

Stephens' general findings, based on several earlier studies, paralleled these. And at his forty-five major institutions Stephens, like Selden for his sample, found differences between public-controlled and other institutions. At the public the average was 5.6 years; at the private, 7.5 years. Selden's averages, however, were all greater than Stephens', being eight years and upward for each of the several classes of institutions according to their control. Interestingly enough, there seems to be little difference between the average tenures of academic presidents and of the top executives in 600 major U.S. corporations. In 1959, the same year as Selden's survey, *Fortune* (November) reported that of the 1,700 officers included in their study, 52 per cent had been in their jobs less than six years; and fewer than 15 per cent had served more than fifteen years, these figures compared with 50 per cent and 13.3 per cent for the academic presidents.[3]

[1] William K. Selden, "How Long Is a College President?" *Liberal Education: Bulletin of the Association of American Colleges,* 146 (March 1960), 10–11.
[2] *Ibid.*
[3] *Ibid.,* p. 7.

The Presidential Search

How are these offices filled? What educational attainments, occupational experience, and personality traits are considered important or necessary? What age is considered desirable? And, then, how do the men appointed meet with these qualifications? Where did they come from? What are their career histories and administrative experiences? What characterizes the "typical" university president?

The university presidency is a goal which attracts many competitors. If an institution is large and well known, there may be more than a hundred candidates for its presidency. Some of these may be direct applicants qualified by little more than a burning desire to be a president, but most of them will merit serious consideration. Even where there is a plentiful supply of willing candidates, the critical importance of the "right" choice and no mistakes makes the job of finding a president difficult and exhausting. The search not uncommonly takes three or four years. One trustee, whose board had spent more than a year in reaching a decision, said that, compared with "president hunting," his law practice was a vacation.

Most observers of the search and selection process agree that it is a hit-or-miss affair. Even where such practices as political maneuvering and propagandizing for personal friends have been ruled out or minimized, there is no orderly mechanism guaranteeing that all qualified candidates for the job will be considered, that the best of those considered will be chosen. There are many men who would make fine presidents but who remain unknown to boards of trustees. Mainly, this is because there are no reputable agencies that can bring the names of all promising men to the attention of boards. A contributing factor is the lack of formal training programs for the presidency, as a recognized profession or occupational specialty. Also, the presidency has the aura of a position of

48

royalty, for which one must not appear to be striving, but which one must be prepared to accept graciously, as befits those chosen by fate. The applicant who presents his qualifications without invitation from the board may be given consideration, but he suffers an undeniable handicap. In presenting a list of things a candidate should not do in seeking the office, a trustee who had aided in the selection of several presidents noted that very few direct applications were given more than a cursory examination.

Although trustees select presidents in various ways, the most common procedure is to assign a committee to receive and review applications, and to nominate a final candidate or candidates for a vote of the full board. This committee usually starts by making discreet inquiries of other presidents, prominent educators, members of the faculty, friends of the university, influential alumni, and those personal friends of committee members who have traveled considerably. In this way a list of presidential possibilities is composed. The committee then attempts to gather detailed information on the prospects by surreptitious interviews and correspondence with those best qualified to give data on the candidates themselves and on their wives, their friends, their affiliations, and the like. One writer noted that such information is rarely reduced to comparable data, and that the report of the committee to the board is usually in the form of opinions rather than of detailed facts. Most writers agree that the board usually bases its selection on rather inadequate information, and sometimes without clear notions of the type of man it wants, or of the direction it wants the university to take.

Often, a peculiar fact or a particular action of a potential president influences the final selection. It is said that Conant was selected by the Harvard overseers after he appeared, on invitation, before the committee and, with a clear analysis of the type of man needed, urged the candidacy of one of his closest friends. Dodds at first was not even under consideration

49

at Princeton. Then, during the search, he did a very intricate survey of the state's educational system which impressed the board. The famous President Rhees of Rochester University, when he was a young professor of Greek, so impressed the wife of a member of the board at a church social that she told her husband, who told the committee, who, after three prominent educators refused the job, promptly elected him. Pritchett was elected to the presidency of the Massachusetts Institute of Technology after impressing some members of the board with a speech on geodetic surveys. Another president was chosen because he was the only candidate who had not been associated with a school of education. The board thought the previous incumbent had spent too much money on their university's school of education. Still another was selected after inspiring several members of the board with a prayer he offered at a political convention. This was the only feature of several candidates on which the board could agree was auspicious.

In most cases, however, no such denouement presents itself to the trustees. From records of the administrative, scholarly, and occupational experience of several serious candidates, from statements about their health, their politics, their methods of relaxation, and their memberships in clubs and associations, and from the candidates' own views on such controversial subjects as sex, communism, gambling, liquor, desegregation, and foreign aid, the selection committee arrives at the point of inviting one or more prospects to meet with it. The prospective president, his active candidacy having been established by now, may be invited to the campus to speak at a university function, or to be entertained more intimately. In either case, as one trustee put it, "everyone makes a valiant effort to pretend that nothing special is going on." At this time the candidate may be asked to present some of his ideas concerning the duties and responsibilities of a president. He may be invited also to give views on student government, faculty participation in policy-planning, or other matters. And he may be requested to state his ideas on educational matters to some of the faculty, and perhaps to alumni.

Finally, the committee reaches a decision and submits the name of its candidate to the full board for vote or confirmation. In some cases the nominating committee's choice is, in effect, decisive in the matter. In others the selection is confirmed only after approval by the board and the faculty.

This procedure is usually followed in choosing new presidents, but by no means always. The outgoing president may be requested to name his successor, especially if he himself is retiring after a long and successful administration. After Jordan left Indiana University for the presidency of Stanford, the board asked him to name not only his immediate successor but the next three presidents as well. Also, it has been common among the larger universities to call on well-known figures in the educational world to recommend candidates for the presidency. President Nicholas Murray Butler of Columbia was said to have named many presidents during the 1930's; and earlier, in the 1920's, few boards reached final decisions without having consulted the Rockefeller Foundation. More recently, certain officers of the Carnegie Corporation and of the Ford Foundation have come to be regarded as important persons to see when a change in presidents is contemplated. Perhaps the greatest of all consultants was Andrew S. White, the first president of Cornell University, whose recommendations were asked for continually. White, during his administration, personally picked two presidents for Michigan, one for Indiana, one for California, and one for Brown, and suggested the men who became the first presidents of Stanford and Johns Hopkins.

No discussion of the selection process would be complete without some mention of the supposed influence of hidden politics in publicly controlled institutions and of personal campaigning for friends by board members in privately con-

trolled institutions. Of the latter, very little can be said, because it so seldom becomes public. At least one trustee thought
the diversity of the composition of most boards made the exer-
tion of personal influence by their members very difficult and
usually unsuccessful. In publicly controlled universities the
situation is much more complex. Critics of state boards of
control have found it easy to point out governors who have
personally hand-picked the presidents of their state universities with the aid of carefully stacked, docile boards. Perhaps
the most flagrant example of this occurred in 1930, when
Theodore Bilbo, as governor of Mississippi, fired the old and
hired new presidents for the state's three institutions in one
hour. With the approval of a friendly board, he selected an
electric-power-company executive, a real-estate salesman, and
a recently graduated schoolteacher to administrate the state's
system of higher education. Other examples have frequently
been cited. When President Stoddard of Illinois, who had
been installed during the governorship of Adlai Stevenson,
resigned in 1953, he indicated that changes in Illinois politics
were the main cause of his termination and would be a potent
factor in the naming of his successor.

One study of 110 state-college and university presidents
revealed that 88 per cent stated their political affiliations
as identical with the governors of their respective states.
Stephens' survey of seventy-six presidents of state colleges and
universities indicated that fifty-three, or almost 70 per cent,
agreed in political affiliation with the governors of their
states. It is probably safe to assume that governors who can
control their state universities' boards of trustees can—and
usually do—influence the selection of state-university heads.

The extent to which politics affects the selection of a president in a private institution seems to hinge on the political
awareness of the board and its members' experiences with
previous presidents or the quests therefor. Certainly most
boards tend to be conservative politically, and can reasonably

be assumed to prefer "safe" men. As one trustee phrased it, "I don't care what party the man belongs to, but we do want to know that he subscribes to the basic economic, social, and political thinking of our country."

The Attractions of the Presidency

Why be a university president? Considering the almost notorious insecurity of the office, its multiple responsibilities, and the great demands made on the incumbent's physical and mental health, one might wonder what makes the job so attractive. That it is attractive is indicated by the number of candidates who appear for every vacancy—both as unabashed seekers of the office and as "available educators," who carefully guide their careers to be ready if the lightning should strike. Some presidents, it is true, have had the mantle of greatness thrust upon them unwillingly, but their number is probably small. Despite the tendency of presidents to consider themselves helpless respondents to constituencies that would not be denied, most seem to have accepted their calls after only the briefest pause for reflection. A. Lawrence Lowell wanted the presidency of Harvard badly, and admitted that he worked for it, pushing himself forward in every activity. In contrast, President Millikan of the California Institute of Technology did not seek the office but acceded, grudgingly, after a member of the board pledged his entire fortune to the institution's endowment fund. President Adams of Michigan is reported to have been "more than a professor" before his election, and was ever ready to serve on committees, "taking a deep interest in the physical plant, the library, financial affairs and the general welfare of the university." One president thought most candidates are men who have risen doggedly, slowly, and consciously from the ranks, accepting each position of greater responsibility somewhat regretfully, as a step away from scholarship, but accepting it, nevertheless.

Most writers believe at least three features of the university presidency make it desirable in spite of its dangers to the incumbent. First, it commands a relatively high salary—the highest in the academic world, excluding some professor-practitioners, professor-consultants, and the occasional authors of best sellers. Second, it is a position of undeniable prestige and access to influence. Third, it is—for want of a better word —challenging. To the ambitious man with a sincere desire to do something for education, it affords a rare opportunity to innovate and to be of unusual service.

In a study of salaries paid in 1952–53 in 417 colleges and universities, the National Education Association's Research Division found that the median presidential salaries for the nine different categories of institutions studied ranged from $7,500 to $18,000. It should be noted, however, that a substantial number of the colleges and universities in this study were small—i.e., had less than 2,000 students. The salary range for presidents of institutions of over 5,000 students is, of course, considerably higher. In a 1948 survey of twenty universities with more than 5,000 students, the presidential salaries ranged from $12,000 to over $30,000. Most changes in the presidential salary range since 1948 have no doubt been increases, not decreases.

Of course, the salary of a president, particularly of a major university, is not his only income. Customarily, he is provided with a rent-free house (the traditional "presidential manse"), a car, and occasionally a staff of servants. In addition, most of the larger institutions provide separate expense funds for travel and entertainment. The salary and extra benefits, naturally, diminish as the institution's size and resources decrease. Nevertheless, when the income of a president is compared with the incomes of his teaching and administrative staff, it must be considered one of the lures of the office.

As there are only about 1,800 colleges and universities in the nation, the position of president is, unquestionably, one of distinction and public recognition. To most citizens, the president *is* the college or university, and as the institution's fame and prestige grow, the prestige of the president increases accordingly. College and university presidents are automatically eligible for *Who's Who*. Their opinions and advice are sought, and usually published, on almost any subject. They are appointed to innumerable national, regional, and state boards, committees, and foundations. To a man, they are embraced by the Elks, the Masons, the Rotarians, the Civitans, chambers of commerce, country clubs, and Indian tribes. Locally, they are leading citizens; nationally, they are leading educators. Moreover, the president is generally recognized as the incumbent of a demanding and difficult office. By those at all familiar with the number and diversity of the qualifications sought in candidates for the office, the president, by virtue of his appointment, is regarded as a man of extraordinary ability. This initial esteem may soon wear off, but even the worst of presidents retains the grudging respect due one who has attained a hard-to-get position. Although presidents rarely admit that prestige is the *primary* attraction of the presidency, most of them agree that it is a factor of considerable importance.

Although some presidents admit that considerations of salary and prestige influenced their decisions to accept the office, a great majority, it seems, believe they were impelled by less sublunary motives. Being a position of power, the presidency has frequently been sought by persons dissatisfied with certain aspects of higher education and sincerely desirous of initiating reforms. For others, it presents an opportunity to improve the quality of a beloved alma mater or increase an institution's stature in academic circles. Still others have sought the job with the stated intention of serving youth and ensuring a strong and virile culture. A few presidential candidates probably are afflicted with Messianic complexes and confuse the interests of the university with their own. To these, the challenge of the presidency is that of fulfilling one's personal destiny. But, to the typical candidate with a deep and sincere interest in higher education, achieving the presidency means his first real chance to create a major program or build a lasting institution.

The Men the Trustees Want

Stephens' study quotes a Yale trustee who commented thusly on the election of President Griswold:

He had to be a leader, a magnificent speaker and great writer, a good public relations man and fund raiser, a man of iron health and stamina, married to a paragon—a combination Queen Victoria, Florence Nightingale, and best dressed woman of the year—a man of the world, but with great spiritual qualities, an experienced administrator who can delegate authority, a Yale man and a great scholar, and a social philosopher who has at his fingertips a solution to all of the world's problems. I don't doubt that you have concluded that there is only One who has most of these qualifications. But, we had to ask ourselves—is God a Yale man?

The truth in this rather wry observation is more often tragic than humorous. When the ideas of what makes a good president are distilled from the writings of trustees, alumni, state legislators, faculty members, and students, the figure that emerges is hardly identifiable as human. Exceptional presidents have usually been discovered by accident, and the ideal president has never existed. The president, ideally, should be all things to all men. He should have wisdom and experience enough to lead a faculty into making decisions with unanimity, but be able to delight the students with his youthfulness. He should be able to take a stand on any public issue without offending either conservatives or liberals, to keep a winning football team without coddling athletes, and to go out and find money while keeping close to campus affairs. Lowell noted that a president was supposed to combine the qualities of a trained seal and a matinee idol with those of a foreign diplomat and an educational statesman. Another president pointed out, gloomily, that the incumbent is expected to excel in so many different and unrelated fields of activity that he is almost certain to fail in some and be abused: he may be an outstanding scholar but a poor orator or tactless fund-raiser; he may be exceptional in those three areas but lack business sense or administrative ability.

An analysis of writings about presidential qualities by members of various groups that relate to the president, or that participate in his selection, reveals several interesting facts. Perhaps the most important is that there is very little agreement on the essential qualities. For example, opinions are about evenly divided as to whether an academically trained man is likely to be a more effective president than one with experience in fields other than higher education, such as business or the military. Many trustees think the most important qualification for the presidency is what has loosely been termed "promotional ability"—including, generally, political acumen, shrewd and aggressive fund-raising ability, vitality and youthful alertness, and sound business sense. To these trustees, whether or not the candidate is a scholar is regarded as secondary—indeed, as having little to do with his probable effectiveness as an academic administrator. An example of such a president, according to one writer, was President Harold Stassen of the University of Pennsylvania. His assets included an impressive record of public-relations work, a mildly liberal outlook, skill as an organizer, a reputation as an energetic spokesman for youth, and a splendid physique. Some critics insist that managerial and public-relations talents are now more valued by trustees than educational-leadership abilities. The changing character of endowments, the varied nature of university business operations, and the tremendous budgets seem to demand efficient and practical enterprisers. Proponents of such candidates would delegate the president's authority to administer certain internal matters and to control educational policies to a presidential associate or a vice-president.

A majority of board members, probably, are still wary of the non-academic man. Most of them agree that administrative skills and promotional abilities are important qualifications. Nevertheless, they seem to favor the candidate with a reputable, if not outstanding, academic background. Unacquainted with the faculty, and usually with no more than a superficial knowledge of the institution's educational activities, the trustees must lean heavily on the president's counsel in educational matters. Most seem to feel that the president should have a real appreciation of the problems of scholarship and teaching and relatively long experience as a student, teacher, or academic administrator. Stephens found their views reflected in the words of a provost of the University of California:

How can anyone who has not lived in the academic world . . . be any more than a Charlie McCarthy when he talks of educational aims and purposes? . . . What reasons have we to anticipate that men, whose aim has been the winning of primaries . . . battles . . . or increasing the earnings of stock-holders, will automatically sympathize with the ideals of a university?

Faculty members almost without exception regard outsiders as generally unqualified to fill the presidency. They usually say that the non-academic president succumbs too easily to demands for travel and for non-educational activities; too often administers through channels, lacks a genuine interest in teaching and scholarship, and is apt to become a mere figurehead.

It is rather significant that the academic-non-academic-qualifications question is nothing new for selection committees. In 1906, President Andrews of Cornell University warned that the appointment of assistants to help the businessman president handle educational matters could not replace a true appreciation of the efforts of scholars by the president himself. Others pointed out that the non-academic executive too often judged performance in quantitative terms, and treated the faculty as some sort of appendage of his personal enterprise. On the other hand, as long ago as 1898 the value of the successful-promoter type of president was being argued. Similarly, trustees and presidents who noted with alarm the increasing growth and complexity of university operations saw in the experienced administrator and successful entrepreneur the only hope for an affective and efficient organization. Wrote one president: "The *executive* president is the latest and best type and we may safely follow his lead in training men for the job."

That this disagreement over proper presidential training continues seems to indicate rather clearly that the bases of selection range widely, and that more variety of background may be indicated here than for other executive positions. Yet, specific occupational and educational experience by no means complete the list of presidential prerequisites. Conscious of the numbers of presidents who yearly succumb to hypertension, heart disease, and general fatigue, trustees consider vigorous mental and physical health of fundamental importance. Although this is not primarily a matter of birthdays, most selection committees seem to prefer age ranges, roughly, between forty-five and fifty-five years. Apparently their theory is that even an outstanding man requires ten to fifteen years to achieve or demonstrate maturity and ability as a scholar and at least another five years to gain experience as an administrator.

Various qualifications of temperament are also considered important. Perhaps the one most often cited is patience. Harvard President Charles Eliot was reported to have pronounced it "the prime virtue of any administrator." Robert Hutchins at Chicago thought patience a snare, and an all too common attribute of administrators. Others have emphasized the necessity for tolerance, sincerity, and integrity (the qualities most mentioned by faculty members), and for a sense of humor.

59

The ideal president is usually pictured as one who knows when to be and when not to be patient, and who is tolerant but not too tolerant, just but not squeamish, urbane but not sophisticated, and, as one trustee put it, "with enough sense of humor to digest his dinner after meeting with a recalcitrant alumnus, but not enough to find the rhetorical clap-trap of commencement unbearable."

Though a few bachelors do become presidents—Indiana's esteemed Herman Wells, for example—it is generally assumed that the president will be married, and it is true that candidates' wives are considered before final decisions are made. The presidency being the kind of office it is, the president's administrative affairs are perforce entangled with his social life, and trustees are well aware that the president's wife can be either an asset or a liability. Thus, she can help keep the faculty indulgent through her thoughtfulness, and can play an important role in the social and charitable activities of the university; but, if she is overly ambitious, domineering, unconventional, or tactless, the president's relationships with his faculty, or within the community, may be seriously hindered. Moreover, the responsibilities of the president's wife are diverse and exacting; her job as hostess and entertainer is particularly demanding. One wife has written that it is not unusual to have a thousand guests at a reception, ten or more house guests (mostly trustees and potential donors), and twenty for dinner—all within the space of forty-eight hours. As it is rare for a president to have chosen his wife while under scrutiny for the office, most trustees prefer "to look her over too" when a new man is being selected. One very highly regarded candidate is said to have been dropped from one board's list because his wife remarked to a committee member, "I just cannot stand reception lines."

Most universities require particular qualities of hopeful candidates before they are considered at all. These qualities, of course, vary greatly, and are sometimes peculiar to the institutions involved. In time they may change with changes in boards of trustees. Some universities are required by statute to select alumni as their presidents. Others are subject to legal or informal stipulations about regional or state residency. Still others require membership in particular churches. As noted earlier, training in the ministry was for many decades considered the premier qualification of a president. Educational experience, scholarly attainments, and administrative abilities may also be qualifications particularly required by a university, or stipulated in its charter or bylaws.

The Men the Trustees Get

Boards of trustees search for supermen. They appoint human beings. And this is the case however great the distance may sometimes seem between lesser mortals and the occupants of that prestigeful office, the academic presidency. Who are these human beings? Having seen what the trustees want, now consider, briefly, what they get in respect to age, prior occupation, education, and other characteristics. The presidents surveyed include those in office in 1960–61 at eighty-eight large universities (over 5,000 enrollment), including Stephens' sample of forty-five; plus 182 other presidents the same year at institutions of less than 5,000 students, but classified as accredited universities or liberal-arts colleges by the U.S. Office of Education. Data on the 270 presidents were got from three standard listings, as well as from Stephens' original dissertation and the studies referred to there. (Details of method and four tables may be found in Appendix A.)

The *median age* of all the presidents surveyed was 55.7 years. Heads of private universities of more than 5,000 students were 57 years median age, two years older than those at large public universities. There is evidence that the median age for large-university presidents has been increasing slightly. Our data show less than one-fourth (24 per cent) under 50 years of age, whereas a study of 52 leading state-university presidents in 1930 had found that over half were under 50. In 1938, the presidents of "300 of the more important colleges and universities" were found to have a median age of 52.5 years. Then, a 1946 study of 812 presidents of "major colleges and universities" found a median age of 53 years.

The *median age at inauguration* of the presidents of our 270 colleges and universities in 1960 was 46.5 years. When the presidents of the 34 member institutions of the American Association of Universities back in 1900 had been inaugurated, they were 41 years old. Their successors 20 years later had been 47.8 years (median) when inaugurated. Other studies of the median age of inauguration have reported 45 years (in 1946) and 43 years (in 1929), but samples and sources were different.

No sure conclusions can be drawn from such a mixture of studies. About all one can say is that there is some indication that presidents are somewhat older now than formerly, and also that they are somewhat older when inaugurated. To what extent this simply reflects the increased life span of our total population is a question.

In *occupational experience,* 66 per cent (58 out of 88) of the large-university presidents in 1960–61 were one-time professors with academic-administration experience: that is, "professor-administrants." As between large universities, public and private, 73 per cent of the presidents in the former and 60 per cent of those in the latter had been professor-administrants.

Those presidents with no administrative experience could be found predominantly at the small, private, non-denominational colleges and universities—as could those who had been former clergymen. Public-school administration figured in the backgrounds of one third of the presidents of small public institutions, but only in one tenth of the heads of large public institutions.

Contrary to popular belief, the proportion of presidents selected from occupations outside higher education does not seem to have increased materially since 1900. The decline in the number of ex-ministers was most pronounced before the turn of the century, as was noted above, and it has continued as a trend. Significantly, only four ex-ministers were found in the 88 major universities of the present study: two in public and two in private institutions. Similarly, the proportion of presidents selected from government, politics, private business, law, and the military has shown no significant tendency to increase.

As the university grows in size, the clearest trend is the increasing emphasis on administrative or executive, particularly university, experience. In the large universities, there seems to have been less change in this respect, comparing 1900 and the present, than there has been among the small institutions. The latter have changed most, though all show a tendency to increase the percentage of presidents with administrative experience in higher education. Indeed, some observers believe a definite presidential career-pattern is emerging, along with the bureaucratization of higher education. That is, the "typical" university president seems more and more to be a professor who has risen through the university hierarchy, from department chairman to dean to provost or vice-president to president. Our 1960–61 survey lends support to this view. Fifteen of the 88 presidents of large universities came to their offices from the presidencies of other institutions, in every case a smaller and less influential college or university. Another 20 assumed the presidencies of their institutions after holding the post of vice-president, provost, or dean of faculties, in their own or other institutions.

In *educational background,* the tendency for presidents to arrive at their positions through a more or less predictable career line is linked with changes in both amount and type of educational preparation. Our 1960–61 data show that 53 (60 per cent) of the 88 presidents of the larger universities had earned a Ph.D. or its equivalent (e.g., Doctor of Medicine, Doctor of Sacred Theology). Of all 270 presidents, 143 (53 per cent) had earned a Ph.D. or its equivalent. Back in 1900, of the 34 presidents, only 9 had earned a doctorate; whereas in 1950, 20 had earned that degree. Other studies reviewed by Stephens showed that of 192 presidents in 1929, 69 (36 per cent) had earned a Ph.D.; and of 300 presidents studied in 1938, 129 (43 per cent) had earned a Ph.D.

As to academic specialties in 1960–61, 45, or about one half of the 88 large-university presidents, had specialized in education, business administration, or one of the social sciences. The social scientists were the most numerous: 26. Educationists and humanists figured in 22 (11 each), and administrative specialists in 8 (7 in private non-denominational institutions). In the small universities and colleges, where 102 of the total of 182 were private denominational, it is hardly surprising that 43 of the presidents came out of theology. For all 270 presidencies, the four most frequent educational backgrounds were, in order: social science, theology, humanities, and business and public administration. The social scientists had 35 per cent of the large public presidencies; 21 per cent of the private presidencies, both large and small; and 18 per cent of the small public presidencies.

With regard to educational background, then, social scientists are the most likely presidential choices, according to our data. If business and public administration is considered social science, the likelihood is even greater. A related conclusion from Stephens' review of earlier studies is that since 1900 academic presidents have been recruited from an ever wider range of educational specialisms. No longer do law, theology, and languages dominate.

For rough descriptive purposes, we may now develop, from the foregoing and from other data in Stephens' monograph and the 1960–61 survey, a *composite picture of the "typical" major university president.* He is between fifty-four and fifty-seven years old and has been in office for not more than six years. He was born and reared in a small town or medium-sized city in Indiana, Illinois, or Ohio. He received his under-graduate degree from a liberal-arts college of less than 2,000 students in the East or Midwest. He earned one or more graduate degrees from Harvard, Chicago, or Columbia. He majored in economics, history, or English. He began as an instructor in a relatively large university; moved up to a full professorship; became a department chairman at a less influ-ential institution; moved up to become dean of arts and sciences, or left to become dean of some other college; was then selected for vice-president—perhaps at a third institution; and, after two or three years, was elected president. He re-mained for no more than ten years in any one administrative position.

He is a Phi Beta Kappa, a Rotarian or Kiwanian, a Re-publican, a veteran of World War I or II, and an American Legionnaire. He is a bank director or trustee of a boys' pre-paratory school—perhaps both. He has served on a state or federal committee. He is a thirty-second-degree Mason. He is an Episcopalian, Methodist, or Unitarian. He is married and has two or three adolescent or grown children. He lists fishing or golf as his favorite hobby, and has been abroad several times. He has written at least one book in his field of speciali-zation, and occasionally contributes an article to a professional journal or popular periodical, usually on higher education. This, then, is "prexy."

Some Concluding Generalizations

The university presidency is an unusual office—unusual, perhaps even unique, in the ways in which its incumbents are selected, in the factors that determine what qualifications are sought in candidates for the office, and in the diversity of these

65

qualifications themselves. Certainly it can be said that one does not train for the position. Some have said that presidents are almost never chosen on the basis of proven competence for the job. Indeed, one writer cites the case of a man who was offered, in succession, three presidencies, each of which called for entirely different qualifications. Moreover, there is very little agreement as to what type of training would be most effective. Yet, several generalizations about the qualifications sought in presidential candidates can be made on the basis of the literature pertaining to the trustees and presidents of the forty-five universities in Stephens' sample.

An important factor in the qualifications sought is the *educational circumstances* of the university. As a rule, trustees are aware of the unique educational characteristics of their institutions and chosen presidents accordingly. Thus, each institution has unique sets of educational problems, traditions, methods, and objectives, and the type of president suitable for the University of California might fail miserably at Princeton. Indeed, this unhappy prospect seems the more likely when one compares the concepts of President Kerr (California) and President Dodds (Princeton). Kerr, from his mushrooming "multiversity" of seven campuses and more than 60,000 students, thinks this is the time for presidents who can mediate between many "sects," "sub-universities," and power centers. He sees the need for general administrators whose specialty is co-ordination: the day of "the giant university president" is past.[4] But Dodds, though he notes a decrease in the "giants," says that educational leadership is the primary need and that presidents should spend 50 per cent or more of their time on purely educational affairs.[5] These conceptions, of course, reflect the differences between California and Princeton as well

[4] "Education," *Time*, May 3, 1963 (Latin America edition).

[5] Harold W. Dodds, *The Academic President: Educator or Caretaker* (New York: McGraw-Hill, 1962).

66

as between Kerr (the economist and labor mediator) and Dodds (the scholarly humanist).

The *current administrative needs* of the university are another important influence on the qualifications sought in candidates for the presidency. It has been said that every university undergoes twenty-year presidential cycles. An energetic scholar-administrator is chosen to improve the quality of the faculty to remove or retire deadwood, to intimidate the too athletics-minded alumni by de-emphasizing sports, to change the curriculum, and to raise standards in general. After several years of alumni rebellion, faculty dissension, and public outcry, this president is replaced by a "morale-builder" or a "fund-raiser," who preserves the educational *status quo* but energetically improves the institution's public relations or its physical plant.[6] This description exaggerates, but there is little doubt that universities are organizations particularly sensitive to special-interest groups whose desires are often incompatible. The administrative needs of the university change, and these changes must be taken into account by the selection committee.

Still another factor that helps determine the qualifications looked for is the current board's *experience with previous holders of the office*. This factor is related to the preceding one, the current administrative needs of the institution. Candidates with personality traits or occupational backgrounds that have proven disappointing or unsatisfactory in previous incumbents of the office will probably not be given serious consideration. Appropriately, the selection of the president has been called a "marriage ceremony": the two-party match is made with the hope that the arrangement will be permanent, and the trustees are anxious not to make the same mistake twice. However, many committees disregard changes that occurred during the terms of successful presidents in the past

[6] E. Cummings, "When Is a College President Successful?" *School and Society*, LXXIV (March 1955), 67.

and search for men like their predecessors. Such "staying with the winner" has frequently led to disappointing, if not disastrous, results.[7]

Certain patterns are discernible in the qualifications most desired by committees. Although exceptions will occur, the presidential choice will probably be a man who has an earned doctorate and is recognized in an academic field—whether through teaching, scholarship, or administration. He will have expressed an intelligent interest and taken an active part in the concerns of his own educational institution, exhibiting both executive and administrative ability. He will have an impressive "front"—be a man who looks, talks, and acts "like a president." And he will be known among university administrators, foundation officials, and presidents either as an accomplished or as a promising figure in higher education or administration.

[7] Jesse E. Adams and H. L. Donovan, "Administration and Organization in American Universities," *Peabody Journal of Education,* XXII (May 1954), 340.

4

The Job Inside

Money Man, Academic Manager, Father Figure

The heads of most managed organizations act in two theaters. One is inside their corporations, bureaus, or institutions. The other is outside, where they negotiate with representatives of other organizations. Thus, one often hears top managers speak of their inside and outside work; and sociologists refer to internal and external relations, representational leadership, bicumbent positions, and so on. Few hard walls separate the inside and outside theaters in actuality, though the distinction is sometimes useful analytically. Such is the view we employ in this and the next chapter to describe, following Stephens, the roles and power relations of university presidencies.

The President as a Money Man

The board expects the university president to possess, or to acquire early in office, considerable business ability. Whatever the particular arrangements the trustees make for managing university finances, their representative, the president, is involved in most transactions. He may not have to handle all financial matters, but he is expected to know how. Ultimately, he is held accountable usually for any embarrassments to the institution. Poor judgment or inexperience in business has been the downfall of many presidents, though this is not the only path to oblivion. To appreciate the president's role as financial principal, and particularly the problems and relationships it involves, one must know something of university financial organization and operations.

FINANCIAL ORGANIZATION AND ACCOUNTING

The most common type of financial organization found in the large university is the *unit* type, in which all financial activities are centralized under a business manager, a comptroller, or both. Where both offices exist, the business manager is responsible usually for all financial matters, and the comptroller, a subordinate officer, is responsible chiefly for accounting, fiscal reporting, and budget control. There may also be an investment officer, a purchasing officer, a superintendent of buildings and grounds, and several lesser officers —each with several assistants, and each responsible to the business manager, who is subordinate and directly responsible to the president.

The unit type of organization contrasts with the *dual* or *multiple* type, wherein the business officer is responsible directly to the governing board, which he usually serves, *ex officio,* as treasurer. In this type, the president is responsible only for educational matters. Once popular, this arrangement is no longer the preferred one and is rapidly disappearing. Its bifurcation of authority for interrelated financial and educational affairs has frequently led to conflict between the president and the top business officer. Often, the business officer has worked with the board of trustees before the president was elected, is personally respected by the board members, and may appreciate the business viewpoints of some board members better than the president. In this situation, if the president does not guide the business officer in the allocation of funds, salary policies, or other matters of faculty concern, the faculty may come to believe "the business manager is running the university." Once this belief is widespread, the president's position as top administrator of educational affairs deteriorates.

The unit type of financial organization presents difficulties too. Where the business officers lack direct contact with the board, too much may depend on the president's ability to understand financial details and to interpret the university's fiscal position to the trustees, or to the budget committee of the state legislature. Actually, most universities, both public and private, operate under a *modified unit* organization. Here the business manager is responsible to the president administratively, but is responsible directly to the board in his auditing and reporting capacities.

Frequent sources of difficulty for the president both in financial planning and in his board relations are the philosophy of finance and the absence of standardized procedure in the university for keeping financial records. Accounting practices in most large universities tend to vary a great deal, and sometimes this results in financial reports that are as doubtful in significance as they are complicated in form.

The accounting and records systems of most universities are modifications of those used in large business enterprises. The latter are geared to give executives maximum information about profits, the changing values of stockholders' investments, and the values of present assets at current market prices. Such accounting systems tend to emphasize profit-and-loss statements, the balance sheet, and careful inventories of current assets. In contrast, the social functions of the university make it a *spending* organization and not a profit-making enterprise, a fact that faculties delight in reiterating. Financially, the aim of the educational institution is to spend whatever income is required by educational and research activities. Funds in most universities are carefully budgeted so as to balance income and expenditures, and, to the responsible educator or diligent faculty member, budget surpluses may be as embarrassing as deficits. After all, a surplus reveals that more might have been done than was done.

In further contrast with the well-managed business, the proper university does not aim to accumulate net assets to enhance the value of original investments. Again, the success of an educational institution is measured by the way in which it spends its current funds for educational services. The fact that many of the larger universities have accumulated capital assets means only that they are capable of (and should be) producing more services than smaller institutions. By such criteria, the profit-and-loss statement and the balance sheet are less significant than the operating sheet that records incomes and expenditures in respect to actual services rendered. Moreover, inventories are useful mainly as guides to the purchasing agent, rather than as expressions of prime wealth. Donors expect not a financial return but a return in terms of services rendered, and these are not easily measured. Records of current assets according to market values mean less than a record of the uses to which funds are being put.

The presidents' relations with their boards and business officers tend to be strained by such differences in money philosophies and practices. Even where a majority of board members know their university's objectives and are dedicated to the institution's welfare, their criteria of successful university administration will often incorporate ideas of productive efficiency, prosperity, and growing assets. But the university president tends to be a businessman in the way that a hospital director is a businessman. He is committed, as educator and chairman of the faculties, to conducting the business side of a philanthropic organization instead of a profit-making business. The more the institution's services increase, the greater is his deficit likely to be at the end of the year if his institution is privately controlled and supported. State universities, with their appropriations, do not ordinarily show deficits.

The usual subsidiary enterprises operated by universities are in fact commercial activities. The financing of housing facilities, bookstores, dining halls, and laundries cannot be managed in the same spirit as that of the educational program. Generally, the students are expected to pay for these services, and administering them requiries careful regard for profits and losses, inventories, and other prudent business considerations. This further complicates the university's accounting procedures, and both helps and hinders the president in his dealings with his board, or with the budget committee of the legislature.

The legislature's budget committee is a principal fact of life to the state-university president. Its image of university finances and its actions being so important, the temptation to ensure a favorable impression at appropriation time by manipulating the university's financial picture is no doubt great. Because of the uniqueness of university accounting requirements and the absence of a standard evaluation procedure, such manipulation has been possible, though dangerous. Some state-university presidents, for example, have been known to treat some transactions and record some data with an eye more to political expediency than to careful accounting.

Boards of trustees sometimes request outside auditors to inspect the financial affairs of their institutions. The reports of these auditors usually go to the board along with the reports of the business manager or the president. Taken together, these are friendly, collateral reports, but constitute a check, nevertheless, on the university's administration. Some boards, however, have asked the auditors to examine the fiscal management in extraordinary detail. These outsiders come to the university as investigators—as likely enemies—instead of helpful critics of the administration. Most presidents have resigned immediately when confronted with such demonstrations of "no confidence" by their boards.

INCOME, ENDOWMENTS, AND INVESTMENTS

Endowments are no longer the primary source of income for the large university. The annual total income of higher education in America grew from about $5 million in 1880 to more than $5 billion in 1960, but the proportion from endowments decreased during that period from 55.4 per cent to 3.6 per cent.[1] Most private universities now find their support mainly in the diversified annual giving of corporations, private foundations, alumni, and friends; in tuition and fees; and in research grants and other income from the federal government. Public universities, of course, continue to be largely supported directly by tax appropriations.

Most large universities still have sizable endowments, however, especially the private institutions that had their greatest growth around the turn of the century. Managing these endowed funds is a financial activity of almost all governing boards.

Harvard is perhaps the only university that has turned over the handling of its entire endowment account to an outside investment company. The president of this corporation, however, was subsequently appointed treasurer of the university. Only rarely can a president remain unaffected by his board's endowment policy. Some presidents are less conservative financially than their boards, and where they are powerful enough to impose their will, considerable controversy may develop. In other situations, the president may find himself caught between board factions holding contrary views on investment management. To restore board peace, or to give the victory

[1] U. S. Department of Health, Education, and Welfare, *Statistics of Higher Education*, 1959–60, chap. iv, section 11, pp. 3–4.

to one of the opposing factions, the president may be sacrificed.

The presidents of universities with large endowments have been known to opt for the national economic *status quo,* and thereby safeguard their universities' investments, presumably. And though one can imagine that a university, for example, whose portfolio featured oil-company stocks might support research on substitutes for gasoline, it is likely that other research proposals would receive a better hearing. State universities, it should be noted, are not immune to such forces. For example, the president of a state university in a hog-raising region was reported to have reorganized the home-economics department after it was discovered that vegetable shortening instead of lard was being used in baking recipes. All circumstances considered, it is hardly surprising that so many presidents lean to the right in politics and economic philosophy. All in all, the decreasing reliance on endowments may well be a gain for university freedom, other contingencies being equal.

THE PRESIDENT AND THE BUDGET

The responsibility for the budget is the president's, a fact of the greatest importance in university power structures. Final decisions on the allocation of funds among the several schools, divisions, departments, and functions are most particularly the president's alone. The budget document itself is prepared by the business staff. Its items and their relationships are worked up from two sides, the business and the educational. The business staff assembles the expenditure and income programs for the top administrative offices, plant operations, and auxiliary services. At the same time, the deans of instruction, in consultation with department heads, prepare statements of expenditure needs based on expected enrollment and other factors. The provost or vice-president consolidates these school and department expenditure programs, often meeting with the deans in a body to review the estimates of needs. Finally, the business manager, the provost or vice-president, and the president get together, combine the educational and business statements, and reach an agreement about an equitable allocation of funds.

If the estimate of needed expenditures exceeds expected income, as is usually the case, the president must decide whether income can be increased. If not, he must decide what proportion of available funds should be appropriated to which divisions of the university. The budget committee of the board then reviews the budget, and may suggest new sources of income or certain reductions in expenditures—rarely, however, raising questions about particular school or departmental appropriations. Finally, the president submits the budget to the full board. If it is in balance, approval is more or less routine. If it is seriously out of balance, reducing expenditures, raising fees, and other steps are considered for bringing expenditures into line with income.

Budget decisions, after the consultations are finished, cannot well be shifted to others; "the buck stops here"—at the president's desk. Important to the success of the educational program is the president's ability to develop a budget that judiciously allocates income among general administration, instruction and research, libraries, auxiliary services, maintenance of the physical plant, and other non-educational activities. Moreover, he must not only decide the allocation of available funds, but must also be able to anticipate future income. Will there be legislative cuts? Will income from endowments decrease? What will be the effects of inflation? of deflation? of war? The president, to meet this responsibility, often moves from the role of administrator or educator to that of promoter and politician.[2] Thus, it is not surprising that

[2] It should be noted that the budget rarely remains stable, but usually increases annually, and at such a rate that the president stays preoccupied with the reaction of the legislative committee, declining interest rates,

annual budgets become yardsticks for boards of trustees in judging the administrative abilities of their presidents.

FACULTY RELATIONS AND THE BUDGET

The officers most involved in budget deliberations are the president, the provost or vice-president, the deans, and the department heads, on the educational side; and the business manager and other administrative officers, on the business side. The general faculty, through committees, may be consulted occasionally about salary policy or promotions, but, as a rule, it gets its information on the budget process through hearsay and rumor.

The part the general faculty plays in financial affairs, especially in the formulation of the annual budget, is determined largely by the president himself. Many presidents prefer to keep the determination of financial matters confidential, for several reasons. Some think budget preparation through faculty committees is woefully inefficient and "trouble-producing." It simply takes too much time. Others believe the teaching faculty member is not qualified to judge the financial claims of the various departments and divisions. As a member of a particular department, the professor has a vested interest; he has neither the time nor the opportunity to get the detailed "overview" of university affairs that the higher deans and the president acquire. Finally, some presidents believe public knowledge of budgetary matters lowers faculty morale and stimulates gossip and interdepartmental jealousy.

In practice, the presidents of most large universities formalize the budget-making process to the point where faculty members, if they are not active participants in the making of decisions, are at least not mystified by the decisions made.

---

demands for salary increases, investment problems, and new sources of income. See O. C. Carmichael, "What Makes a Good College President," *Bulletin of the Association of University Professors,* XXXIII (November 1947), 685.

Each dean or department head, for example, usually feels that his unit should be allocated funds commensurate with the amount of service (and income) it is producing; increases in enrollment should mean increases in resources, and so forth. Under some presidents, this system is strictly adhered to. For instance, Conant at Harvard became known as "a slide-rule administrator."

Some presidents encourage deans and department heads to become promoters and fund raisers—to establish individual relations with trustees, corporations, government agencies, foundations, and the like, who may earmark funds for specific educational purposes. This may cause trouble for the president as co-ordinator of development and educational programs. Such promoting and "empire-building" tends to give power to those deans or directors whose subordinate departments have "salable" products. This is power not only to increase the national stature of the institution but also, and more immediately, to strengthen the demands of the deans in such matters as faculty recruitment, salary increases, promotions, and the allocation of physical facilities. This power correspondingly weakens those in the university who possess equivalent official responsibilities or other potentials for power but have no departments to promote. A case in point, characteristically, is the dean of the graduate school. He has on paper the authority to develop graduate work and research in the university, but in fact he does little more than play clerk and record keeper to graduate students and busy professors. Several deans, and even some department chairmen, may outpull him in the power struggle.

These contests and conflicts, these plans and power alignments, can make presidents into harsh patriarchs or indulgent parents, judges or servants of faculties. Most presidents seem to think their control of the budget, and hence of the purse strings, enables them to maintain a balance between the power they can exert and the responsibilities assigned to them by their boards of trustees. Even so, the ingenuity and determination of deans and faculty are sometimes such that a school of medicine or business, for example, comes to dominate a university, and the other divisions become mere appendages or service agencies—the president having been unable to prevent it.

Most presidents complain that their financial decisions are especially harrowing and are a source of some disillusionment. Typically, the president comes to feel that he is constantly saying "no," and all too often unwillingly. It is especially hard to refuse a dean or department head additional resources when his unit has brought additional income to the university. Faculty who have heard the expansive, pro-academic talks of their presidents—while they were being wooed to join the university, at commencements and other occasions—are often shocked when their requests for funds are turned down. They are shocked all the more because they are certain their own requests were the most worthy imaginable. Consequently, "to lie like a college president" is not an uncommon phrase in the academician's lexicon. Fortunately, the president can fall back on his board of trustees. He can always deal with a request he does not want to refuse in person by saying, "Well, I'll take it up with the board, but I'm sure they will turn it down and this inopportune request may jeopardize a timely one later."

The President as Academic Manager

Asked for his opinion of the new president of his university, a professor said, "I don't know anything about him, but I hope he has enough sense to let the faculty alone." We do not know how widespread this attitude is, but the statement points up two basic aspects of the university presidency: extensive delegation of responsibility for educational management, and effective tenure by faculty sufferance.

The American university with an instructional staff of 500

or more has a number of faculties, schools, and lesser units organized on the basis of educational subject matter, as we have outlined in Chapter 2. The president of the university, by delegation of the board, is responsible for co-ordinating the efforts of all faculties and departments, for recruitment of their staffs, for promotions and dismissals, for the distribution of funds to each, and for the maintenance of an adequate standard of instruction. These administrative responsibilities are usually further delegated by the president to subordinate officials—vice-presidents, deans, and department heads—as he sees fit. It should be emphasized that the delegation of presidential responsibilities varies considerably from one institution to another. The trend, though, has been toward more co-ordination at lower levels—toward more delegation of presidential responsibility to subordinate officers or faculty committees.

There is one responsibility, however, that the president is not expected to delegate. It is one of the few presidential charges, moreover, for which boards also delegate clear authority. This is the task of planning, interpreting, and effectuating major educational expansion and contraction. Contrary to the mistaken idea of many faculty, the president is rarely the trustees' "front man," carrying out edicts and siding sycophantically with wealthy board members, in conflict with the faculty. More often, the board looks to the president for direction. Typically, they hire him because they have acknowledged his ability to plan for the future and because he has specific plans in mind. As one president put it, "They back him up and continue to back him up—even in mistakes—until he has made too many, and then they get rid of him."

Presidents are sensitive to the attitudes and opinions of their boards or legislatures. This is quite understandable, for they need only remind themselves that it was their boards that appointed them and gave them what authority they have, or that it is their legislatures that hold the purse strings. Nevertheless, "prexy" is more than a managing director and simple employee. Having been elected, he is an associate member of the board and the only person given the privilege of formal initiative in the internal administration of the university.

THE FACULTY'S PART IN ACADEMIC MANAGEMENT

Though trustees delegate little clear authority to the president, he tends to wield much power, especially over educational activities. The president's power derives mainly from his control of resource allocations—not least, money—and from his authority to initiate changes in educational programs. The extent to which presidents share this power with their faculties and administrative colleagues has long been debated. As noted previously, faculties do not as a rule play an important part in the determination of financial policies. Educational matters are another thing.

Most major universities have executive councils composed of administrators and faculty. Such a council, characteristically, is advisory to the president on educational affairs. Usually, the president initiates major policy considerations within the council, which may then report to the faculty.

The general faculty usually participates in a deliberative body, commonly called the senate. This body sometimes includes all administrative officers and full-time faculty. More often it includes only the university's administrative officers and full professors. Occasionally, however, it is a body of elected representatives of the several schools, divisions, or departments. Ordinarily, the senate's responsibilities are rather routine: determining graduate requirements, recommending candidates for degrees, approving curricula and calendars, granting awards and scholarships, handling student discipline, and the like. Occasionally it may be consulted in the selection of deans, and even of a new president. The senate usually operates through its own standing committees or committees appointed by the president. The numbers of these committees vary; in the larger universities there may be twenty-five, thirty, or more. In some places almost every faculty member belongs to at least one such committee.

Through their executive-council representatives and through committees of the senate, then, university faculties participate in educational-policy and general-administrative decisions. The extent of this participation varies considerably. Historically, it has not been very great. The power of the faculty has been chiefly the *liberium veto* over considerable proposals of the president, of other administrative officers, and of elements of the faculty itself. Such veto power and veto groups are realities of academic administration.[3] They confront and parry both the board's legal authority and the president's—and sometimes the deans'—more visible power. Although the president, in turn, can veto almost any faculty decision, he must stay more or less in tune with the faculty. He may solo now and then, but eventually he must fall in with them if they refuse to go with him. As President Harper of Chicago pointed out years ago, the president, through the power given to him by the board, may easily become a despot—browbeating people, making and breaking careers. He cannot stop "progress," however; he can only stand in its way.

Why, even with the concessions made by boards and presidents, have faculties seldom formed legislative or administrative bodies that *initiate* major policy considerations? There are several reasons. First, there is almost no tradition of collective action among faculties in American universities. Only on matters of academic freedom and of tenure have faculties, as collective bodies, organized and asserted strong convictions. Second, administrative and committee work, faculty meetings, and discussions take too much time from scholarship, teaching, and leisure. Third, most faculty members are so individualistic

[3] There is a penetrating analysis of veto power and veto groups in David Riesman, *Constraint and Variety in American Education* (Lincoln: University of Nebraska Press, 1956), pp. 53–106.

and so concerned about their own specialties that they are seldom interested in broader university issues. Fourth, leadership is often not there. Leaders in name do not necessarily command respect by academic standards; they may be mere spokesmen for the president, or for influential and powerful department heads. Also, chairmen who believe democracy is synonymous with "free discussion" sometimes waste time and create frustration. Fifth, and finally, faculties possess few sanctions. Therefore, some ask, why "act like" responsible legislators? As a consequence of this collective inadequacy, most faculty influence on the president and the board continues to be exerted by individuals, and the faculty member's first loyalty continues to be to his department.

Many professorial spokesmen object to the power of the university president. Generally, the president is the faculty's only recognized communication link with the board of trustees, but often there is no assurance that he will recognize a primary loyalty to the faculty. After all, the board, not the faculty, chooses the president. And too often, according to the faculty, this choice turns out to have a Jehovah complex—refusing to confer with his associates, impatient with opposition, vain, ostentatious, infallible, and, above all, lacking in educational leadership. At the same time, more and more academicians seem to agree that administration by faculty committees is neither practical nor desirable. The multiplicity of problems involved in financial matters alone—in budget preparation, the investment of endowments, the securing of legislative appropriations, and the like—would be exceedingly difficult for committees to handle.

At the same time, many faculty members think presidents could use the composite experience of their professors far more than they do in making educational and financial policies. They would like to have much more voice in faculty promotions and salaries, in budget appropriations, and in matters relating more directly to the educational program. Accordingly, many urge more faculty representation on the decision-making bodies—and not just on the executive council but on the external board of control itself. They want a surer way of informing the board of their views, both on internal administrative policies and on the selection of the president who will lead them.

Today it is a rare president who has not expressed himself as favoring some increase in faculty participation in the administration of universities. Some matters, like faculty recruitment and the advising of students, are often solely in the hands of the academic departments, with the president and his administrative officers only exercising formal approval. Recently, presidents have tended to involve more faculty members in their educational planning and, in some cases, even in budget matters. In these developments, the professors' best friend has often been the foundation official, who was once a professor or academically sensitive president himself, likely as not, and whose big money now sanctions his polite suggestions to boards and presidents.

Most presidents, however, feel that where they and their administrations are held responsible, they should in fact be responsible. The university is complex, and the intricacies of compromising numerous faculty viewpoints demand a centralized authority. This authority, moreover, should not be vested in groups whose interests are involved. The president commonly sees himself as above the vested interests of departments, alumni, students, etc. He thinks he sees the university as a whole and is responsible for its over-all growth and success. Such responsibility demands commensurate power.

Presidents often find it difficult, sometimes impossible, to identify faculty members willing to sacrifice specialty interests to general educational programs. Policy determined by the faculty is apt to be dictated more by personal power concerns than by institutional needs, and thus lead inevitably to dog fights between deans and departments—to the world of the knife and the hook. Moreover, policy-making by faculties can be stultifying when they are able to resist any innovation as a threat to a secured position. The reluctance of faculties to accept changes in educational programs is a reason frequently cited by presidents for their skepticism of more faculty government. When professors point to the democratic governments of such universities as Oxford and Cambridge, which theoretically are owned and operated by the faculties, presidents are apt to reply that such institutions have tended to develop an almost irresistible force for the maintenance of the *status quo,* and are covered more with barnacles than with ivy.

As to faculty representation on boards of trustees, presidents have generally taken the dim view. One referred to meetings between representatives of the faculty and of the board as perfunctory and pleasant social functions that accomplish little and are a fifth wheel to the president. Another president, asked about faculty representation on the board, was reminded of the Soviet Politburo's hamstringing authority by appointing commissars. No executive with integrity or self-respect could countenance this, he thought. On the other hand, back in 1911, President Schurman of Cornell urged, in his annual report, that at least three members of the board be from the faculty.

THE PRESIDENT-FACULTY CONFLICT

Some presidents who were professors have found themselves regarded adversely and suspiciously by their erstwhile colleagues. To such faculty members, the very fact that a professor has turned president is evidence of his vanity, his thirst for power and public notice, or his impertinence as an educational statesman. At last he has revealed himself as a cormorant and a Machiavelli. Though such views are held by a minority, perhaps, presidents and professors are commonly reserved and restrained, if not suspicious or antagonistic, in their relations. This is partly attributable, of course, to the authority and power relationships already discussed, and

85

partly to differences in salary, style of life, age, and prestige.

It has been suggested that even though the president no longer inspires the awe and fear of a magistrate dispensing life or death, he is still a formidable figure to the average faculty member. The professor frequently trembles at approaching the president. He feels inferior, and resents it. A nod of approval from prexy may elicit an exaggerated response of appreciation; a lifted eyebrow or frown may stifle overt disagreement. This type of relationship, in a professional who prides himself on being an individualist, may by its very nature breed disgruntlement and unexpiated feelings of inadequacy.

Many presidents believe that under these conditions they are bound to be the chief target of blame—for low salaries, for heavy teaching loads, for a faculty member's failure to produce research, and even for the nation's foreign policies. Like stomach ulcers, such criticisms are the symptoms of internal tensions—produced in this instance by the modern university system. One writer insists that this "natural antipathy" between the president and the faculty is the source of most professorial criticism, particularly that which belittles the administrative task (e.g., "Anyone can be a president") or accuses the president of insincerity, a desire for personal aggrandizement, or ignorance of educational values. This antipathy is reflected in faculty humor, which sometimes has it that the assistant dean is a mouse, the dean a rat, and the president a fat cat. In such situations—by no means universal, fortunately—the new president easily runs afoul of the faculty's discontent, and occasionally stumbles into open conflict. This is the more likely because there is no mediating body. The board typically has neither the time nor the understanding for heading off such disputes, which may very quickly turn into major crises.

Also, the president as a personality may exacerbate the latent misgivings of the faculty. Often a new president knows less about the internal management of the institution than many of the faculty. Furthermore, a majority of them may be at least his equal in educational attainments, and outside his own specialty everyone outranks him as an expert. Often, of course, a president is selected for other than academic accomplishments, and many of the president's duties bear no direct relation to education. Financial problems continually assail him. Politicians, alumni, students, parents, businessmen, and various civic enterprises and organizations give him little respite. If his interests in education are at best tepid—if he buries himself in routine or spends most of his energy improving the physical plant or working with the legislature—he soon loses the confidence of his scholars. As one outstanding president noted:

The temptation to bury oneself in routine is tremendous. There are so many reports, so many meetings, so many signatures, so many people to see—all that have some value to the institution, that you can conscientiously draw your salary and never administer at all.[4]

The president is expected to sustain and encourage the efforts of the faculty, who have taken the vow not only of classroom and laboratory but—as compared with him at least —of poverty as well. Nothing irks the scholar quite so much as the president whose interests center on finances and who seems to consider the faculty a necessary but not very economical appendage of the university—that is, of himself, the buildings and grounds.

Much of the conflict between the president and the faculty arises because innovations are so often originated by the administration rather than by the faculty. New departments and institutes, even new schools, are created; major realignments or readjustments are made; curriculum items are added, abandoned, and changed. By and large, the faculty is likely

[4] R. M. Hutchins, "The Administrator," *Journal of Higher Education*, XVII (November 1946), 400.

to view such changes with alarm or skepticism, especially when they bring new competition for funds, and the tendency of most faculties to resist changes that affect promotions and tenure has already been noted. Thus, presidents frequently complain that the merits of innovations are too often ignored because of faculty self-interest.

If a president is tactless or authoritarian while, for example, trying to raise teaching standards or eliminate deadwood, he is almost certain to provoke a tempest over academic freedom or traditional faculty privilege. Ordinarily, the president is kept unaware of his mistakes by the power inherent in the presidency: he overrules unwittingly; his casual opinions stifle protests and smother debate. Such presidents, despite their motives, seldom outlast the faculty members who are only going through the motions.

Not even under the most favorable conditions, however, can the president keep on good terms with the faculty if they lose confidence in his honesty or integrity. Because the welfare of faculty members depends so much on the character of the administration established by the president, they are sensitive to his every opinion, viewpoint, and statement. These are weighed regularly and examined with great care for signs of inconsistency, ignorance, or lack of courage. Rarely is the president successful in juggling policies and pronouncements so as to please at once his faculty, the alumni, and the general public. Especially is this true in the state university, where the president represents an institution that is expected to be a grateful beneficiary of public funds. In facing outside pressures, state universities too often lack endowments and traditions such as enabled Harvard's president, in 1949, to tell a self-appointed inquisitor to go to hell; and Washington University's chancellor, about the same time, to encourage the resignation of a board member who opposed a professor's signing a civil-liberties petition. Yet, the president, however unwillingly, is expected to defend faculty freedom; and if many faculty suspect the president of intrigue with groups outside the university, or think he is prepared to sacrifice any principle for more funds, acute estrangement or open conflict may develop. In fact, disputes over academic freedom or violations of tenure are frequently cited as the most common causes of open conflict between presidents and their faculties.

CONFLICT AND POLITICS IN THE FACULTY

Even where the president has been able, by means of persuasion, sympathy, and unbending courage, to gain the respect of his faculty, he still faces the exhausting task of getting faculty members to accept one another and to work together. Divisions of opinion strain faculty relations in most universities. Departments disagree about the boundaries of their areas of knowledge; professional schools compete for funds; ambitious professors dispute points of method, theory, and fact. Conflicts within and between departments often grow out of personal dislikes, and power politics are played by administrative officials and influential faculty members. Thus, it is not surprising that the political maneuverings of a Tammany boss are said to be as tame as a church social compared with the fights waged by faculty members for power or position in the large universities.

Such power plays and antagonisms may become as destructive to the president as conflicts between himself and the board of trustees, especially as academic presidents suffer a disability shared by few other chief executives: so many members of their administrative cabinets and staffs are legacies from predecessors. Commonly, they vary widely in age, experience, viewpoint, ability, personality, and loyalty. Unusually critical is the university president's ability to either unite divergent interests or replace officials gradually through retirement or "acceptable" terminations. Here the difficulty is that university officials so often expect and enjoy tenure of office and promotions in grade according to academic principles. The result is that the chief executive's hands are tied; he cannot choose his own staff as he might like and as he can in other kinds of organizations. The university president who dares bring in appointees of his own choosing from outside does so at considerable peril.

Frequently, the president must take a man as dean or for another office, not because he has proven competent, but because he is a valuable faculty member who must have a salary increase; or because no one else can be persuaded to assume the burden of administrative detail. Where there are different salary scales for professors and administrative officers, some presidents think it is too often the mediocre faculty members who can be lured away from scholarship to keep records or to soothe anxious or irate parents. These conditions tend to encourage the efforts of faculty politicians. Would-be deans jockey for positions on committees, apples are polished, and skillful administrative officials line up followers. Rather than political maneuvering in faculty assemblies, most campus activity of this sort seems to take the form of exerting personal influence on the executive power.

As noted previously, so many of the president's conversations with the faculty are about money and conclude with a "no," he is apt to be blamed even when it is faculty politics that have denied the ambitious. Few presidents can afford the luxury of moderating all faculty disputes, and few receive adequate information about *sub rosa* politics. The president is too busy. He is often away from the campus, leaving such matters to the vice-president in charge of faculty affairs. He attends few committee meetings, usually depending on his agents for information; consequently, he often receives only summary reports of the actions taken, and only partial ideas of the sentiments prevailing, at the meetings. Too often, members of committees are mere names to him, and the committee work impresses him more as time-wasting than as productive. Moreover, presidents tend to believe they should avoid personalities and ignore ever-changing faculty alignments. Theirs is the duty, instead, to "stir up a comatose department, clear away the debris of out-worn traditions, and push forward new plans—pleasantly if they can, unpleasantly if they must." Not a few seem to agree with President Jordan, the first chief executive of Stanford, who advised academic presidents to avoid the cliques and differences of opinion of faculty members by never letting them get together except once a year and then shutting their mouths with a long address.

The President's "Perfect" Faculty

Despite the strife, conflict, and politics—noisy or quiet—it is a rare president who fails to include in his public utterances some reference to the well-rounded, brilliant group of scholars who constitute the instructional staff. There are no weak links. If the world were scoured for the most trenchant thinkers and rutilant personalities, it is doubtful whether a better faculty could be assembled. Privately, both the president and his faculty know that this accolade is mostly a promotional "pitch," or a product of commencement or inaugural euphoria—in any case, not to be taken literally. Faculties are never perfect; they all need periodic pruning.

To be informed on professors' individual abilities, to evaluate their performances, to replace the incompetent, and to keep the best are probably the most difficult and unrewarding tasks of a president. Most of the responsibility for faculty personnel in the large university, as we have noted, is delegated by the board and the president to the various deans and department heads. As a rule, the president comes to know faculty members only superficially and in an impersonal way. A few distinguished scholars or teachers may emerge as distinct personalities, but the majority of faculty members are virtual strangers to him. Yet, he must evaluate the qualities and the services of the instructional staff. Each budget raises this problem anew, however it is handled. It must be decided whether to retain instructors without permanent tenure or notify them of termination. Who among them are promotable and who are not—and when? Shall an ambitious associate professor be promoted or the risk be taken of his leaving for greener pastures elsewhere? Is it better to retire or replace the professor whose work is unsatisfactory but not bad enough to compel dismissal? What is best for the university? What is fair to the man? How can any dismissal (where tenure is involved) be accomplished without bitterness on both sides?

Such decisions are extremely difficult. There are no sure ways of measuring teaching competency. Even if there were, the president would have to get his information through channels that might distort it. Too often he accepts the judgments only of those who have his ear, or he uses his own chance impressions, or relies upon numbers of applications or ratings by students or alumni—thereby making it difficult for himself to promote or replace justly. Moreover, some faculty members become avid salesmen of themselves. By publishing non-controversial books, by becoming institutional show-pieces, or by making themselves useful in myriad administrative ways, they are often able to create impressions of great competency.

Having decided to dismiss a professor, the president faces the hazards of making the decision stick. Almost invariably he is expected to consult the faculty, or a judicial committee thereof, if the man has tenure. But, even with the approval of this body, he may risk an investigation by the American Association of University Professors. Few presidents relish this prospect, both for the adverse publicity it would bring and for the implication it would carry that the administration is tyrannical and unjust.

That some administrations have been so can be judged from the position of a former president of the University of Vermont, who, in his maiden speech to the faculty, announced:

(1) he would be keeping a close eye on them; (2) he would tolerate no criticism of his policies; (3) he would begin immediately an investigation to clear out deadwood; (4) he would hire and fire as he personally saw fit; and (5) he would fire the first man he caught taking a drink—or, as he put it, "working as an iconoclast in the beautiful temple of youthful ideals." No wonder presidents seldom handle satisfactorily the problems of insuring their universities' academic standards. The necessary decisions are easy to postpone, and boards of trustees rarely initiate consideration of them.

The President and His Students

To most university students, the president is the remote and peripatetic figure who occupies the middle chair on the commencement platform and at other times is busy about mysterious financial doings, public relations, and affairs of state. The president may be interviewed frequently by campus editors, athletic managers, and student politicians; but his direct contacts with other students are limited mainly to an occasional talk, special dinner, or reception. Usually, most communication consists of written pronouncements relayed through deans or other administrative officers. (One new president of a women's institution, though, communicated in rather a novel, perhaps risky, fashion. He sported a pocket kerchief over his heart on which was sewed, in red, "I like girls." This relationship contrasts sharply with the era when the president taught every student at one time or another, and sometimes even knew each member of the graduating class by name and reputation.

Several have observed that the president tends to regard the student as an incidental statistic. In the press of operating and expanding a multi-million-dollar enterprise, some think, the student is treated as a product to be assembled in four years at minimum cost; then to be packed attractively; and, finally, to be placed in the labor market as an income producer eventually for the university. At best, this observation is erroneous; at worst, it is a deliberate exaggeration. Few, if any, presidents fail to recognize that, though the university is a congenial setting for the advancement of faculty research, it is even more a center for higher learning. It exists because of and for the students, and its justification can be based on little else. Moreover, most university presidents seem honestly to deplore and regret the demanding schedules and responsibilities that prevent them from establishing more intimate bonds between themselves and the students. The most unapproachable president gives more thought to student problems and needs than many think. Few financial or educational policies are unrelated to student affairs or activities; practically every decision the president must make will affect the students, directly or indirectly. Furthermore, many serious student matters that, for various reasons, are unreported are settled quietly by the president, who receives little public credit therefrom, even though blame comes notoriously easy.

The criticism that presidents too often think of students in quantitative terms and as potential donors occurs partly because presidents and their faculties occasionally disagree on what a higher education should include. Because tuition, student fees, and alumni contributions are important income sources, and because university finance is a major part of his job, the president tends to be more sensitive than the average faculty member to student preferences in educational content. For better or for worse, the university must maintain a satisfied clientele in order to prosper. At the same time, it must compete rather fiercely with other universities. The president not only must offer prospective students the things they want; he must somehow convince them that they want the things the faculty would like to teach them. This concern with the choices of students is even more pronounced in modern universities, especially the public ones, which are expected to

94

meet the needs of diverse citizen and special-interest groups. The power of the student to influence changes in the educational program and his effect on the economy of the American university have resulted in a tendency toward the development of academic department stores. This tendency, along with its implications of subtle control on presidential policy-making, was noted years ago by a visiting German rector, who predicted many of its deleterious effects.[5]

Although president-student relationships tend to be remote and indirect, the president traditionally stands in *loco parentis*. Most presidents sense an obligation to see that the students are well served and, perhaps more important, that the interests of their parents are promoted through the university. Students and their parents tend to regard the president today as a more or less disinterested party, responsible for almost everything, whereas formerly they considered him a representative of the faculty.

The president's father role should not be minimized or ignored. This role is to be found in the largest and most bureaucratically organized institutions, as well as in universities where faculty members and students alike have sought father substitutes in their presidents. Even though the president typically sees little of his students in primary, face-to-face relationships, his very presence often is of great significance. A personal word of greeting to a student is ordinarily seized upon, treasured, and repeated with appropriate embellishments.

The president who is careful to remember names and who is quick to respond to the father-role expectation typically enjoys an enthusiastic, if somewhat exaggerated, student popularity. This does not necessarily entail a "door-is-always-open" policy. The essential quality is the manifestation of a sincere and somewhat protective personal interest in student

[5] Aloi Brandl, "Personliche Eindrucke von Amerikanischen Universitan," *Deutsche Rundschau*, CXXXI (April 1906), 127–9.

95

affairs and problems despite pressing university matters. The "father" is perceived to be very busy, but he should not be too busy to play with his sons and daughters occasionally. The paucity of presidents who have been truly revered, in the sense that they have elicited expressions of personal esteem and affection, indicates the difficulty the president faces in meeting the expectations of his demanding office. The presidents who have enjoyed the most affectionate responses from students are those who have remained long in their office and are no longer plagued by the insecurities of office. To be relaxed, patient, and cordial with students, however, is probably more difficult for a man whose very job may hang by the thread of day-to-day decisions.

5

The Job Outside

Public-Relations Man and Educator

In contrast with the mumbling professors who seem to pursue the esoteric and forget their overshoes, there is the president as seen by the trustees and the public. He stands trim in his executive suit, young in spite of his fifty-odd years, a figure with both feet on the ground and a big proposition to put over. In his outside theater, the president is expected to play a major part in the promotional activities of the university—educational statesman, winner of friends, and attracter of money. Of such is "the job outside." And the tools are those of public relations and fund-raising, no matter what other terms may be preferred in the halls of ivy. Institutional goals must be stated and interpreted, goodwill must be generated, available services must be advertised, visitors must be welcomed and entertained, controversial professors and misbehaving students must be hidden or explained away.

The President as Public-Relations Man

Public relations is a function variously handled in the large universities. Sometimes it is divided among several administrative offices and co-ordinated by a public-relations officer. Often a number of public-relations and publicity experts are retained as promotional and development staff to operate carefully planned programs. One such development program was said to feature P. T. Barnum's showmanship, David Harum's shrewdness, and Elsa Maxwell's magnificence. No matter the staff, however, it is the president who is expected to be the most potent salesman. And it is the president who is most sought out as a source of information. He cannot isolate himself from all the people who want to see or hear him render an account of the university.

The president's office is flooded with mail of every conceivable sort from all kinds of people—requests for contributions and sponsorships, advice and opinions on administrative policies, demands for appearances and speeches on any topic from dirt farming to foreign policy. One president noted with dismay that he was beginning to compensate for his paper-thin knowledge in some areas by increasing the fervor and conviction of his delivery. And then he realized he was about to convince even himself. Most trustees expect the president to devote considerable time to public-relations activities. He is expected to make and maintain contacts with government, foundations, clubs; and to carry out a public-speaking program of some magnitude. He should attend important alumni dinners, hold receptions for distinguished guests, entertain visiting legislators, introduce speakers, serve on various committees, and publish an occasional article. According to one study, most presidents of large institutions delivered between forty and 100 public addresses a year, met with alumni groups between six and fifteen times a year, and published between one and three articles a year. Many of these speeches and dinners necessitated trips outside the state. Somehow the president must decide which commitments to honor and which to ignore. His choices will reflect, and also determine, the relative importance of "the inside job" and of academic matters in his thoughts and energies.

COMMENCEMENT AND THE HONORARY DEGREE

Once a year the pageantry and pomp of commencement draw to the campus a throng of proud parents, sentimental alumni, national dignitaries, perennial attenders, and loyal friends of the university. Typically, it is an occasion of satisfaction, sentiment, and well-being—a time of renewed friendships and recounted memories. It is the day the university dons its robes of ceremonial dress, proclaims its traditions, and recalls to the public its ancient heritage. The value of such a spectacle for the winning of friends and future donors is seldom lost. In most universities, the staging of a proper commencement has come to be a matter of great importance in the public-relations program. As one writer has said:

The old era of commencement programs—with student orations, faculty speeches, presidential addresses, and individual presentation of diplomas is almost gone . . . The object now is to stage a ceremony with sweep and pageantry. Colorful processions, great masses of black-gowned candidates, acres of spectators, and a stately, traditional ritual create an exciting spectacle. It is the greatest academic show on earth.[1]

Where the president still makes the major commencement address, he will usually sum up and emphasize all that the university stands for and is trying to do. Occasionally, a more omniscient president will launch into a denunciation of totalitarianism or regimentation. Or he may analyze the social, political, and economic health of a nation. Whatever the subject, these pronouncements are almost always intended to

[1] G. B. Wilson, "Commencement at the Large University," *Journal of Higher Education*, XXIII (February 1952), p. 93.

point up the university's importance to the public. Partisanship is carefully avoided, and any political utterances tend to be conservative and carefully related to academic matters: the threat of higher taxes to endowment income, investigations and academic freedom, and so forth.

It has been suggested that a subtle way for the president and the board to express a political opinion, though maintaining an official neutrality, is by means of the honorary degree. Certainly, the list is not always identifiable with present or future achievement. One study of the honorary degrees conferred by 500 institutions over a period of twenty years found the honoree most apt to be selected to be (1) of the "right" politics, (2) an alumnus, (3) a generous donor, (4) the personal choice of a board member, or (5) another president.

Most presidents seem to think the honorary degree has been overworked as a public-relations technique. None, however, is willing to suggest any drastic changes in the practice. Actually, it is rare that the degree in major universities is blatantly put up for sale, and it serves many useful purposes, not the least of which are prestige, publicity, attraction of commencement speakers, and academic courtesy. Then there is the honorary degree as a source of faculty humor: for example, what the University of Kentucky president is supposed to have said to that great horse, Man of War, when he came forward for his commencement honor.

THE PRESIDENT AS RITUAL HEAD

Not only at commencement does the president play the ritual leader. As one president said, "Regardless of his age, prexy is *ex officio* the oldest person in the university." The president personifies the university; as its leader and head he represents the authority and voice of ten centuries of academic tradition. He presides over all major university functions. It is by the authority vested in him that all candidates receive their degrees. Much of his traveling time is devoted to appearances as the representative of his university in the ceremonials of other institutions—centennials, inaugurations, anniversaries, and the like. It is for this reason that he is expected to "look like a president." Whether in the front-row center or at the head of the academic procession, his presence is expected to be dignified, remote, overpowering, and a little exalted. The meaning of this role of the president is most clearly defined during his inauguration ceremony. There is an air of inevitability and royalty about this event—the impression of great powers being transferred and a destiny fulfilled.

An inauguration is no relic of an outworn tradition. It is something much more vital . . . it marks the crucial significance of leadership. . . . the president's . . . role is fixed by an inexorable law of nature. On him depends the destiny of the organization he leads until he dies or resigns.[2]

This ritual leadership of the president has had, and continues to have, an important influence on the public's conception of his office. There are presidents, for example, of many organizations from the national government on down. But it is significant that only the college and university administrator is given the informal title "prexy." It has the flavor of emotion, intimacy, a term of paternalistic affection. To the public, the president is generally presumed to be the fount of all knowledge, moral, far-seeing, honorable—a good and Christian man. This expectation sometimes conflicts with the demands that he be a promoter and administrator.

DONORS AND FUND-RAISING

Once upon a time university fund-raising in the United States was mainly personal solicitations of large gifts and emotional platform appeals. Commonly, the approach was

2 S. P. Capen, "Relation of the State College to the New Movement in Higher Education," *Educational Record*, XI (January 1930), 15–16.

on the basis of charity. Hoary institutions teetering on the brink of foreclosure called for support from all loyal and thinking citizens. Tycoons were courted and convinced. Rich and elderly invalids suspected of testamentary thoughts were carefully cultivated. It was an era of urgent requests and ten-million-dollar bequests. Whole universities were philanthropically tendered as gifts—Cornell, Stanford, Johns Hopkins, Duke, Chicago, Vanderbilt, Rochester, and Carnegie Institute of Technology. To beg like a college president became a byword. And the great presidents of the era, with the possible exception of Eliot at Harvard, were indeed selected for their phenomenal ability to attract resources. Until George Eastman was convinced by Rush Rhees, his interest in the University of Rochester was luke-warm, John D. Rockefeller could not refuse the request of William Rainey Harper at Chicago. Both Jordan of Stanford and White of Cornell were veritable magnets for funds.

Today fund-raising by large universities is a different matter. There is much less dependence on the "big donor" and endowment support: the primary sources of income are parents, alumni, foundations, industrial corporations, and federal aid to education. This has resulted in a definite change in the character of appeals. Universities offer resources and services —educational, scholarly, and vocational—that are attractive and salable. They represent safe and unselfish opportunities for investment. They are necessary for the expansion of a specialized, industrial civilization. Solicitation on the basis of charity? Of course. But it is charity born of reason, and solicitation by staffs of specialists. Lawyers and tax experts are engaged to point out investment possibilities to corporations; brokers and counselors advise on behalf of the university; the great fraternal organizations have been recruited.

More and more universities assign most fund-raising activities to a separate office with trained personnel selected for that purpose. In addition, private firms of fund-raisers may be employed to build and conduct special campaigns. Yale, Cornell, Harvard, and many others have separately organized departments of financial promotion, designed to relieve the president and his executive associates of part of a burden which must distract from the administration of internal affairs. The officer assigned to head such an organization generally works directly under the president and is given a variety of titles: "development officer," "financial secretary," "field agent," and sometimes "vice-president." Whatever the title of such an assistant, the fund-raising activity tends to be centralized and under the immediate direction of the president.

Recently some universities have decentralized fund-raising, making each major dean responsible for promotion of his own school. The thought is that no president, even with a specialized staff of assistants, can speak authoritatively of the needs of medical, theological, legal, dental, and engineering education. Such decentralization has led, in some cases, to complaints by deans that they are becoming salesmen unable to devote enough time to educational policy matters within their schools.

Trustees of larger universities are frequently accused of seeking presidents who are promoters and who possess the glamour necessary to attract money. There is no evidence that this is any more the case now than formerly. However, there is little doubt that the president's success is often measured by the money he attracts. To fulfill his promise as the man with a plan and a program for "greatness," the new president may easily be torn between educational development and promotional campaigns. The presidents are rare who have been able to conduct both activities successfully. For the presidents of some of the smaller institutions the choice is already made: they must raise money to survive.

Conflict between winning friends and money and providing educational leadership tends to create tension in the president. The greater his concern over financial needs, the more difficult it is to avoid compromises. Should he overlook the affluent alumnus' efforts to surreptitiously support the star quarterback? Should he accept the large contribution with the small string attached? Should he ease out the professor who continues to bring the institution bad publicity? Furthermore, he must develop a public appeal that may be foreign to his tastes, especially if he has come out of a scholarly career. Often the scholar-president fails as a salesman. The relatively short term of President Glenn Frank of Wisconsin was attributed to his inability to compromise on educational issues and his extraordinary ability to flout Midwestern custom. President Tappan of Michigan soon became an object of loathing by legislators who despised his "codfish accent and condescending manner."

THE ALUMNI AND ATHLETICS

Students graduate, not from the university, but into the alumni association. Everywhere the graduates are organized into associations that seek, not only to advance the welfare of the university, but also to preserve the traditions and spirit of college life. Alumni organizations are a pattern peculiar to American higher education. It is practically unknown in European universities, where it is assumed that when a man graduates, the school is through with him. In Germany, for example, loyalty is restricted to *Korps* or *Burschenschaft,* the student fraternities and clubs; or perhaps to the student's *Verein,* his colleagues within a special field of knowledge. However, neither of these groups involves the graduates. Even among British universities, where alumni often lend financial support, there is nothing like the graduate interest that characterizes American alumni.

With university finance depending more and more on alumni groups, increasing attention has been directed by promotional staffs to their organization and stimulation. Hence it has become almost a prerequisite of the occupant of the presidency that he be able to rally alumni support for the institution. It is up to the president to interpret the needs and practices of the school from which his alumni were graduated. To a greater or lesser extent he must meet with them, court them, and explain to them, not only why their contributions are important to the maintenance of the institution, but also how much they should give and how it will be used. And he must engage in this program personally: brochures and bulletins with their routine announcements, class news, and pictures of dignitaries shaking hands with prexy are not enough. The periodic emotional orgy at the annual gridiron classic and the nostalgia of commencement reunions may tug at the heart strings, but it is the president's personal plea and firm handshake that is counted on to awaken the sense of responsibility and to loosen the purse strings.

The increase of alumni stimulation by the president and the rise of the alumni association are historically coincident with the introduction and expansion of inter-collegiate athletics. Both of these phenomena appeared in the latter half of the nineteenth century and are not unrelated. The introduction of inter-collegiate sports proved to be a great stimulus to alumni, and university officials did not hesitate to use this new interest in their attempts to deepen the relations between the graduate and the university.

As a result of these earlier efforts to encourage among the alumni what has been called the eleven-hearts-beating-as-one attitude, presidents find themselves faced today with an unusual dilemma. For, although it is true that the university has come to have a significant and personal aspect for the graduate never dreamed of a hundred years ago, there is little evidence that the average alumnus thinks any more deeply upon educational aims, needs, and problems. On the contrary, it has been observed that over the past twenty or thirty years the majority of alumni who have gained positions of influence have been chiefly from the ranks of those whose interests lay more on the emotional or athletic side of university life than on the thoughtful side. This tendency led one president as far back as 1912 to remark somewhat bitterly:

The Alumni are no longer scholars or even professional men. They are more interested in football than the serious work by the university. Any university club today could get along better without its library than without its bar.[3]

As more money is solicited from alumni, and as more alumni hold definite stakes in the university, it becomes increasingly difficult for the president to ignore alumni opinions when the purposes of the university are being considered. Such pressure can become very strong, and few presidents feel able to avail themselves of a former colleague's advice to "de-emphasize, sell the stadium, and let them howl."[4] Unfortunately, even if the president wins the fight to de-professionalize athletics, or tone down the social life of the campus, he will have made enemies and may be handicapped for the rest of his stay in office.

Hence, it is left to the president to attract alumni support in every way, but, at the same time, to maintain the best possible faculty and offer a sound educational program. These particular objectives are not easily balanced. President Lowell of Harvard, who not only failed to look after the students, but cast a baleful eye upon fraternities as well, is agreed to have suffered more alumni criticism than any other university president before or since. No president reports himself in favor of professionalized sports, for example, but there are those who seem to share what President Hutchins called "the great football fallacy"—that is, good teams will increase enrollment, reputation, and income.

The Midwestern state universities still seem to feature foot-

[3] J. M. Cattell, "University Control," *Science*, XXXV (May 1912), 847.
[4] J. R. Tunis, "Fellow Alumni of Mammoth," *Harper's*, CLXXI (November 1935), 740.

ball and football problems prominently. One Big Ten president, when asked about his private automobiles, retinue of servants, and palatial residence, said:

This doesn't come from state funds—the alumni provide it. All I do is keep a winning team and no scandal. We give the boys scholarships—$500 to $2,000 each and the alumni help out with other expenses. We have tutors to help the boys get through their courses. It's all open and above board—an honest subsidy. I don't understand how the other institutions get into trouble—must be that they don't look after the boys.[5]

At Ohio State an outspoken alumni secretary condemned the football-scholarship policy. The football coach, Woody Hayes, took up the defense and, at the same time, offered advice on higher education in the African nations. *The New Yorker* (January 27, 1962), under the heading "Dept. of Higher Education—Pigskin Lining Division," quoted the Columbus *Dispatch* as follows:

"I see where our alumni secretary is going to Africa," he said. "Well, they think they've had trouble before, wait'll he gets there . . ."

"He is going there to tell their university people how to build a strong alumni association. And if he doesn't tell them they must have a good football team to achieve this he's not telling the truth . . ."

"I feel there is no greater educational function of a university —I don't like the term public relations—than a sound football program. The alumni must have something to rally around . . . and don't think those development funds aren't aided by those 50-yard line tickets," the outspoken Buckeye coach declared.

There is much presidential wordage on the subject of athletics. Professionalism, lack of faith on the part of other university officials, covert methods of alumni, hypocrisy, and deceit have frequently been charged and counter-charged. And through it all the president must listen with patience

[5] Clarence and Mary B. Decker, *A Place of Light* (New York: Hermitage House, 1954), p. 39.

and consideration to the reactions of the old grads who contact him by mail, phone, and personal visit. More than one president repeats the venerable joke about the colleague who wished he were a penitentiary warden so his alumni wouldn't come back for visits. (That president obviously did not know prisons.)

PROMOTION AND THE LEGISLATURE

Since the prosperity of the state university often depends more upon a favorable legislative committee than upon a loyal and generous body of alumni, the state-university president is expected to carry on a somewhat different promotional program from the president of a private institution. Usually such a program is elaborate and strenuous. Seldom is the president expected or willing to entrust it to other hands.

Beginning immediately after the close of one session of the legislature, the president must begin his campaign of public relations and information for the next one. Generally, this amounts to making or maintaining an atmosphere favorable to the university throughout the state. Influential friends of the university must be lined up. Meetings must be held with the alumni, service organizations, parent-teacher associations, and professional groups. Legislators ordinarily are invited to the campus prior to convening to discuss problems and see the physical plant. Budget analyses and other literature must be circulated to the citizenry. It is the job of the president to convince, show, and explain what the university is doing, what it is able to do, and what it would like to do for the entire state. Finances and money are secondary considerations at this stage. It is the educational program that has to be sold.

Recognizing that the most convincing arguments and the best-laid plans may come to naught, some presidents rely upon more direct and effective means of securing a healthy appropriation. As most committees are appointed after the legislature meets to investigate the needs of the university, it is sometimes possible to bring alumni pressure to bear in the committee selection. An influential alumnus here and there within the legislature is a powerful weapon for the president, but a dangerous one if he bets on the wrong horse. One president who gained something of a reputation for packing committees, regularly and painstakingly cultivated the friendship of every young lawyer in the state who showed any promise of being elected to the legislature.

Lobbying by alumni, students, friends, and the president himself is not unknown. In most legislatures both houses have to vote on the recommendations of the committee, and when there is a close party division, much can be lost at the last minute. It has not been uncommon in the past for the president to save an appropriation on the brink of disaster through personal eloquence and shrewd horse-trading. This procedure has also been known to backfire. President Jordan of Indiana suffered one appropriation cut by appealing to a leading legislator he had criticized in a lecture years before while a professor. Jordan had forgotten the lecture but the senator had not, and brilliantly led the opposition.

However, the president's major promotional effort is reserved for the presentation of the university program to the budget committee. The board and the alumni provide him with aid, but it is the president's personal ability to present educational policies and issues persuasively before the committee which usually determines the extent of university support. As it is the president who will be spending the money, he generally commands more attention by the committee than any other official. He must be "sound" through it all. His program must be effective, practical, and, above all, understandable to non-academic people. He must have within reach the answer to almost any question. It did not surprise one president, for example, to be asked by a committee member who had visited the campus why the students in the chemistry building were kept busy "mixing up different kinds of colored water."

The methods and approaches used by presidents to promote university interests in the legislature defy classification. Practically everything seems to have been tried at one time or another. A former president in a Midwestern state, in which the legislature was dominated by rural representatives, regularly appeared at appropriation meetings wearing a patched and musty suit and carrying a red bandanna. Flavoring his address with homespun anecdotes and salty aphorisms, he was reputed to have been unusually successful. Others find the necessity for impressiveness and practical soundness entirely foreign and uncomfortable to their scholarly natures. John M. Coulter, a distinguished botanist and former president of Indiana, said he always felt like washing his hands after a session with the legislative committee because he hated the job of asking the state to support its university. Some have even attacked the problem in a humorous vein. President Cross of Oklahoma, for example, assured the committee that more money was needed because he wanted to build a university of which the football team could be proud. The committee was not amused.

The President as Educator

EMINENT SCHOLAR AND GENTLEMAN

Before the growth of the modern university, it was this role of the president which distinguished him as a public figure. In the average college and seminary of the eighteenth and nineteenth centuries he was a lighthouse in a sea of mediocrity. Typically, he was learned, broadly traveled, urbane, and of irreproachable character. Frequently, as a trained theologian, he had a firm grasp on the truth in all fields of knowledge and on all public issues. He was a man of grave demeanor and deep thoughts—a spellbinder, with the authority of God and the voice of a prophet.

The general public still regards the president primarily as an educational leader. Trustees, in judging presidents, rank "leadership in maintaining the high academic standards" the most important consideration, even though they rely least on "discussion with the faculty" in their assessments.[6] Almost always he is consulted on educational questions at any level, in any context within his own community or state. Leaving the campus, prexy becomes the spokesman of scholars and scientists, the elaborator and interpreter of their work and of the grand plan of higher education. Ordinarily, it is the president who reassures a dubious board of trustees or indignant alumnus that whatever novelties might be dispensed in the classroom, the university is safe from subversion and sabotage. Very often the president finds himself in the equivocal position of encouraging challenging ideas within the organization while he is reassuring the distrustful and suspicious on the outside. More than one observer has noted the half-challenging, half-cautious note that echoes through presidential addresses and annual reports. Science and freedom of thought must proceed untrammeled and unimpeded on the one hand, but ethical and national responsibilities must be observed.

But the public conception seems to go deeper than this. The president is not merely a leading educator; he is a *Christian* educator of integrity and high moral principles. Regardless of what he represents to the faculty, trustees, and students, the president represents to the public that which is good about education. Unlike the controversial professor, the unconventional intellectual, or the seemingly unsuccessful schoolteacher, the president rarely offends with his educational pronouncements. He is not easily swayed by transitory

[6] Tyrus Hillway, "How Trustees Judge a College President," *School and Society*, 89 (February 1961), 51–3.

fads and fashions. Generally, he is not misled by radicals and extremists. His dedication to scholarship is humble and it tempers, for hard-working parents, the flippancy of undergraduate sons and daughters. Above all, the president respects character above degrees. He is almost never an educated snob.

Perhaps it is for this reason that public reaction to the appointment of a non-academic president is often favorable. Although the president may never have earned an advanced degree or participated in research, the public may think him the better for these omissions: the more practical are his educational ideas likely to be. To be sure, he should appreciate the efforts of scholars, but someone has to keep his feet on the ground. Higher education today is big business.

PRESSURES ON "THE POLICY-MAKER"

What, then, *is* the educational role of the modern university president? Ordinarily, he is no longer a dominating personality, giving character and scholarly leadership to an otherwise colorless faculty. He is more likely to be the leader of an executive group and a co-ordinator of scholarship and scholarly resources. His assent is necessary before any fundamental academic changes are made, but many of these policies are group products submitted for his consideration. Though previously a scholar and teacher, his objective now must be to remain in harmony with scholarship and teaching without engaging in these activities himself.

This change in the nature of educational leadership is one factor in the appointment of non-academic administrators. The modern university is no longer dependent upon one man to give it color and individuality. There are few presidents whose philosophies deviate from the main stream of educational thought in America. Rather, there is a tendency toward standardization and the production of graduates who are transferable and interchangeable. There is a premium placed on administrative and executive talent. Conceiving, putting into effect, or enunciating any clear and refreshing view of education may be the least of the president's personal responsibilities. President Dykstra, ex-city manager and hero of the 1937 Ohio flood, who succeeded Glenn Frank at the University of Wisconsin, is quoted as saying:

I gave no inaugural address at the university; first because we had none, at my request, and second because I do not know how to make an educational pronouncement. I did give a charge to the seniors in June and I spoke for 10 or 15 minutes at the first meeting of the faculty. . . . Neither of these talks was an attempt to box the compass in education.[7]

Relatively few presidents, either academically or non-academically trained, have the opportunity to visit quietly and consult with one another or with other learned men about broad educational ideas and policies. Certainly their traveling is extensive, and they frequently talk about education, but to the alumni, the legislators, the businessmen, and at celebrations and centennials. Such pronouncements are often accumulations of second-hand knowledge or mazes of superficialities, or both. All of which leads some observers to believe that modern education, far from being led at all, is guilelessly drifting along the lines of least resistance.

The president, nevertheless, continues to be assigned the formal responsibility for formulating and initiating educational policies. Moreover, he tends to regard himself more of an educator than an administrator and executive expert. Very likely he was chosen for his demonstrated broad scholarship or for his insight into educational needs and problems. The fact that conflicting demands upon his time and energy make difficult any strong and effective personal leadership in educational matters, and requires him to delegate initiating and planning activities, does not relieve him of responsibility, both to the board of control and to his various publics. Conse-

[7] P. E. Sargent, *The Handbook of Private Schools* (Boston: P. E. Sargent, 1937), p. 43.

quently, the president is frequently cast in the role of protector, or supporter of academic values, along with an executive committee or cabinet and subordinate faculty groups. Similarly, it is the president, as the highest authority within the organization, who must ultimately pass judgment on cases involving educational principles, particularly where the issue is that of academic freedom. The president's roles as both defender and judge in educational controversies are inextricably intertwined and must be analyzed in conjunction with one another.

Because the welfare of universities depends upon so many constituencies—legislatures, boards of trustees, alumni, parents, students, and others—the president receives vast amounts of advice, criticism, and pressures with regard to educational policy. The "fundamental purpose" of universities, the needs and nature of higher education, the rights and duties of faculty inquiry and expression—these are matters of continuous controversy, though not always in the open. No one but the president can authoritatively state the position of the university in these controversies. As one president put it, "he is paid to take the rap." The particular stand that he takes will not only affect the character of scholarship and education; it will to a large extent determine the range and quality of academic freedom enjoyed by faculty members.

The tendency for American universities to be sensitive to the social and political pressures of the day has been noted and deplored frequently. Often small but powerful vested-interest groups or bodies of well-meaning citizens have become critical of faculty views on economic, social, or religious matters. Occasionally the board of trustees becomes concerned. Often the alumni insist on a reorientation of university aims and objectives. Invariably the president is accused of either shielding radicals or ignominiously bowing to the wishes of powerful individuals and groups of whatever kind. For the state-university president, this problem is further complicated by the quasi-political nature of his job. Failure to resist these pressures on the part of presidents has frequently been cited as the cause of universities taking on the character of department stores—offering a wide enough variety of goods to please everybody and saying nothing to upset the customers.

As the board of trustees retains ultimate authority over all university affairs, there is nothing to prevent members from taking an active interest in details of the educational program, or asking that an objectional professor be dismissed. Traditionally, these matters have been entrusted to the judgment of the president and his administrative officers, but it would be a mistake to assume that boards exert little influence.

It must not be imagined, for example, that the president's recommendations for changes in the educational program are automatically accepted by the board, or approved after only a cursory examination. Many of the president's ideas may be contested. A biographer of President Eliot of Harvard reports that during that revered gentleman's first twenty years of office the board of overseers maintained a severely critical attitude toward most of his educational policies. On some measures they never did give in. Others were saved only by Eliot's astonishing knowledge of every detail in every department, the exact pains with which he elaborated his points, and his practice of keeping up a constant pressure of comments, arguments, and persuasion until the board broke from exhaustion.

Trustees' opposition to educational innovation is a subject of frequent complaint by presidents. Many consider such opposition an infringement upon their responsibility for internal administration, or as a lack of confidence in their ability to judge educational needs and problems. Whatever his interpretation, the president usually must take a stand. If his recommendations are consistently declined, especially when this means overruling the faculty as well, the president has the choice of championing a great row, or accepting the position of figurehead of the board. While neither of these alternatives is pleasantly contemplated, one is usually chosen before the third possibility, immediate resignation.

The active part some board members take in determining educational policies has been attributed to a number of things. It has been suggested that most board members, being businessmen, tend to lean too heavily on expediency. They have their eyes on the alumni, the appropriations committee, an influential newspaper editor, the House Un-American Activities Committee, or some wealthy donor. Occasionally the board falls under the control of a small but powerful minority that nurses a pet theory or particular objective, or that represents some narrow vested interest. Many presidents believe that the perspective of most board members is too limited, and gives undue emphasis to short-range planning. Currently burgeoning enrollments and the "excess" demand for admissions may be operating to reduce the temptation to stress vocational training or emphasize athletics in order to increase the university's enrollment and reputation.

THE PRESIDENT AND ACADEMIC FREEDOM

Probably the greatest publicity attaches to incidents of board influence in cases involving freedom of academic discussion or tenure. As the board frames, or at least approves, the university personnel policies, it determines to a certain extent whether the climate of the university shall be hostile or friendly to the faculty. Again, it is difficult to ascertain the prevailing tendency of boards in this regard. Incidents in the past seem to have occurred more frequently in publicly controlled than in privately controlled institutions. This has been attributed to the fact that public universities are dependent upon political bodies for support and are more subject to political caprice. Theoretically, both the board and the president are expected to be vigorously active in protecting or defending the principle of free academic discussion on behalf of the faculty. Occasionally the board becomes disturbed by public outcry or alumni pressure and seeks to avoid adverse criticism of the university by dismissing an outspoken professor or demanding a scrutiny of textbooks and course content for subversive matter.

Some writers consider the first two decades of the twentieth century as a particularly dark period for intellectual freedom. The pressure upon faculties to conform to standards set by the board was the subject of many articles at the time. And it was during this era that the Association of American University Professors was organized. Certainly the record of presidents in defending faculty members from attack was not impressive at this time. Only a very few firmly resisted board pressure in dismissal cases, and even fewer carried their resistance to the point of resigning. There is a difference of opinion as to the willingness and ability of presidents to stand up to the demands of board members in cases of academic freedom. The McCarthy period produced enough incidents of both yielding and resisting by presidents to provide ammunition to both sides of this controversy. Cases of dismissal where professors invoked the Fifth Amendment rather than discuss their political beliefs are pointed to with much alarm. Others accuse faculty organizations of invoking academic freedom to protect tenure rights for incompetents and showmen.

Exposed as he is to criticism by the board, alumni, faculty, and general public, the president tends to feel that whatever stand he takes with regard to academic freedom will prove unpopular with somebody, or some group, vital to the prosperity of the institution. His judgment in these cases almost always seems to be based on a sincere desire to do what will be best for the university in the long run, although there seems little doubt that presidents have weighed the value of support they can expect from individuals and groups involved.

It has been suggested that the presidents who have most successfully resisted public attempts to curb freedom of discussion in universities have done so, not because they have received encouragement and support from their faculties, but because they have convinced the board of trustees. Often the president experiences real difficulties in dealing with board members' complaints, because the professors themselves refuse to take an unequivocal position. Too often the colleagues of a professor dismissed by the board restrict their expressions of protest to verbal alarums, or look to the president to hear the burden of argument alone. Few professors who protested the dismissal of Nearing, Dana, Cattell, Watson, Tolman, and others preferred to resign in sympathy. Such success as the presidents were able to record seemed to be gained in spite of the group they were defending. In the words of one more vitriolic observer:

Let the trustees of any university say to the faculty in all honesty: "Go ahead and say anything you like in the classroom or out of it, no matter how radical"—and 99 per cent of the professors would go on saying just what they would otherwise. Trustees . . . are not one bit more conservative or fearful than professors. There is nothing more . . . conservative than the academic mind, nothing so violently opposed to a new idea, nothing that so instinctively shrinks from change. Almost all of them desire only a bigger salary. The trustees desire the *status quo* because they have prospered under it; the professors want it because . . . they want to be left alone to talk about things as they have been. An interest in things as they might be is not part of the academic mind.[8]

PRESSURE BY THE ALUMNI

Like the board of trustees, the alumni seldom have an official voice in educational policy-making, but their opinions are given freely to the president and they must be considered with patience and tact. Ordinarily, the majority of graduates from a given university do not concern themselves with these matters. The destruction of "Old Main" or the expulsion of

[8] Percy Marks, *Which Way Parnassus?* (New York: Harcourt, Brace and Company, 1926), p. 201.

the first-string backfield in the middle of football season may temporarily provoke their interest in the internal affairs of the institution. Though they grumble about the radical element that has infested the campus, few of them contemplate serious action. Sometimes the alumni association, like other voluntary organizations, falls into the hands of a minority that is pointedly interested in the educational program. The point or purpose may be an extension or improvement of the varsity athletic program. Or it may be to press for "more practical education," say, more courses in business. Still others urge the president to eliminate alien doctrines, socialistic textbooks, or radical professors. William Buckley, the author of *God and Man at Yale*, went so far as to state that it is the function of alumni to regulate the educational policies adopted by the university and to ensure the purity of course contents and teaching.

To many presidents, pressure from the alumni is an irritating itch that cannot easily be scratched. President Lowell of Harvard, who resisted all alumni efforts to bring about the dismissal of Professors Münsterberg, Laski, and Frankfurter, suffered a tide of criticism which continued unabated over ten years and spread to all aspects of his administration. Most of this campaign was carried on in public and accomplished little but embarrassment to the president. Frequently, however, alumni pressure is less directly exerted. The president of a state university may find that influence is being used on the legislature's appropriations to curb what cannot be eliminated by direct appeal. Whether or not the president can survive such maneuvering often depends upon his own success in building alliances and winning or check-mating in a power struggle.

THE PRESIDENT AND HIS FELLOW EDUCATORS

Over the past forty years there has been a tendency for more exchange and co-operation among the presidents of major universities, especially with regard to educational policies and pronouncements. Previously, presidents were less willing to do this. If a general policy matter was being considered by a president, he might occasionally seek the opinions of a few presidents or deans who were his personal friends, but such considerations were usually confined to the university family. There were several factors involved in this attitude, aside from the simple inconvenience of getting together or consuming time. Many new universities were beginning to compete for students and funds with older, and sometimes resentful, institutions. The state universities of the West and Midwest stood in sharp contrast to the ivy-encrusted private establishments of the East: in outlook, in philosophy, in practice. Competition was ruthless. And occasionally two or three universities would band together secretly against another on such questions as state appropriations or enrollment requirements. Such conditions did little to foster feelings of confidence and co-operation between presidents. Even the Association of American Universities, which was organized specifically to bring together the presidents of leading institutions and deal with common problems, was a relatively impotent body until after World War II.

Historical circumstance has changed this picture. Perhaps more than anything else, World War II and its aftermath made university officials seek a common front to deal with the problems of veteran enrollments, federal contracting, the draft, and officer-candidate programs. Also, the rapid expansion of all types of professional training, and the emphasis of industrial corporations on a more or less standard type of graduate for their executive positions, tended to reduce differences between public and private universities, with regard to both objectives and needs. The problems of raising money, student admissions, additional plant, government research, foreign-aid programs, and legislative lobbying are problems common to all major universities. The modern university president finds himself a member of a number of associations which come to exercise more and more influence on his educational decisions.

ACCREDITING AGENCIES AND THE PRESIDENT

One factor contributing to the greater standardization of university educational programs has been the accrediting agencies. Originally, such bodies were organized on a regional basis by university faculty and administrative officials to prevent educational malpractice and to assess the value of course credits to be transferred from one institution to another. By withdrawing or withholding accreditation from a college or university, the regional agency served public notice that the institution in question was failing to provide those facilities and programs recognized as proper by most academicians. Such an organization was thought to be needed if any standards of education were to be maintained. Otherwise, a sort of Greshman's law would operate—with worthless degrees and diplomas driving out those of some meaning and value.

These efforts to evaluate the total educational effectiveness of particular institutions have never proved entirely satisfactory. Many presidents complain that accrediting practices are meaningful only in flagrant cases, and the criteria for evaluation are faulty. By measuring hours, equipment, income, and administrative offices, universities can be ranked and judged, but little can be said about the quality of the education they offer. Or, as Henry Wriston of Brown said, "You can't understand the chemical content of a package by measuring the package." Such things as the institution's geographical location, its avowed purposes, its current leadership, or its unique history and tradition are rarely taken into account.

Dissatisfaction with earlier attempts at total evaluation led a number of professional societies—law, medicine, pharmacy, dentistry, engineering, and others—to establish their own accrediting machinery for the purpose of assessing facilities provided for education and research in their fields and to protect standards within the professions. Later, these agencies were followed by accrediting agencies organized by societies representing other disciplines—social sciences, literature, languages, home economics, and so forth—in an effort to evaluate individual departments within various schools of the universities. Today, the number of accrediting bodies which may evaluate aspects of the university program, or the university itself, run well into the hundreds. The effect these agencies have had on educational policies should not be underestimated.

By and large, presidents of major universities are exceedingly unhappy about most accrediting activity. Each agency represents what is, in fact, a vested interest, and it is becoming more and more difficult for the larger universities to meet all their various requirements for accreditation. The president, already beset by problems of allocating scarce resources, is continually faced with the decision of whether or not to risk losing (or seeking) accreditation in one school or department in order to bring others more in line with already existing regulations. Because many of these regulations are relatively inflexible, the president may think that such an elaborate machinery encroaches on the authority of the university officials. The president may even feel himself little more than an agent of accrediting agencies, faced with the choice either of total submission to the system, or of open revolt and the inconveniences that such a boycott would entail.

The open revolt is not more frequent is attributable to the fact that the universities have so often depended on their accreditations. This is true, for example, of income from federal funds. Government contracts by law must be restricted to institutions accredited by the regional associations; and there is also a tendency, unofficially, to consider the accredited credentials of particular schools and departments before granting or contracting as well.

Presidents, as a rule, do not belong to the council or boards of accrediting agencies. Some presidents think this is a fundamental error, especially when it comes to the accrediting of professional schools. Too often, they argue, the accrediting authorities disregard the welfare of the total university in their preoccupation with standards for a professional school. The argument that accrediting bodies give the faculty a weapon for forcing the president and the board of trustees to correct sub-standard conditions leaves the president cold. Ordinarily, he considers himself and his administrative officers better informed than anyone else about the weaknesses or needs of the university. Understandably, he resents the implication that an outside authority is needed to coerce him into using university resources to best advantage.

To curb the authority of the various accrediting agencies, member presidents of the Association of American Universities established a National Commission of Accrediting. When unreasonable standards or requirements were set by a particular agency, the universities, aided by the original *regional* accrediting bodies, would no longer recognize the offending agency. In this way it was hoped that some of the more demanding accrediting bodies would be forced out of business. What this amounts to is the accrediting of accrediting agencies on the part of the nation's leading university presidents, and represents a further step in the direction of stronger relations between university administrators.

PART III

Administrative Style and Its Effects: Succession at the Top of a State University

6

The University of North Carolina before the Change

Up to this point the book has dealt generally with patterns of power, bureaucratic and collegial, in numerous universities and presidencies. Now we invite the reader's attention to a single university and its chief officers in the academic-manager role and, thereby, in interaction with the faculty. The main idea here is that roles are played differently by different men and with demonstrably different effects. And this is the case, particularly, with two presidents who occupied the same office in succession. The differences are those of administrative style: the characteristic manner in which an administrator behaves. One man's style is not the other's. Note that this is *not* just another way of saying, "Individuals have different personalities."

Possibly administrative style can be treated as an item of

personality or temperament, but such a psychological view would not serve the purpose here. Instead, our curiosity runs to sociological phenomena: namely, qualities of human relations, types of power, kinds of skills, methods of making decisions and gaining compliance. These are the key elements of administrative style to be pursued in the next three chapters, drawing on a study of change in top administrators.[1] The objective is to tell what happened when one administrative style was followed by another at a major state university, by means of a chronicle of the situation prior to the change (Chapter 6), the change itself (Chapter 7), and the effects observed four years later (Chapter 8).

Fortunately, we can name the university and the people whose administrative behavior we have observed, a rare privilege in such studies. Our *dramatis personae* were public officials who could see even themselves with a professional and clinical eye. They have recognized the organizational, rather than the personalistic, nature of the study, and they know we are more concerned with universities in general than we are with the University of North Carolina *per se*.

THE UNIVERSITY'S GROWTH AND BUREAUCRATIZATION

The University of North Carolina at Chapel Hill is one of three previously autonomous institutions that in 1931 were consolidated under a president, to whom their respective administrative heads, the chancellors, report. (A chancellor is the equivalent of a president elsewhere.) The other institutions are The Womans College at Greensboro, and North Carolina State at Raleigh—the land-grant institution of the state. The Consolidated University of North Carolina has a single board of trustees of 100 members. They are elected for four-year terms, one member from each county, by the state

---

[1] The research report, as yet unpublished, is available from the author. Selected data tables and details of method have been included in Appendix B, this volume.

legislature. The rivalries between the three institutions, and especially those at Chapel Hill and Raleigh, have been numerous and sharp. Something of the passions aroused in alumni, legislators, trustees, and administrators is reflected in the sequence of official names for the institution at Raleigh: "North Carolina State College," "University of North Carolina at Raleigh," and, in 1963, "North Carolina State of the University of North Carolina at Raleigh." But let us get to the institution at Chapel Hill, the subject of our study.

In 1956 the University at Chapel Hill, the first state university to be chartered in the United States, had an enrollment of 7,300 students and a faculty of 517. Its chancellor was Robert B. House, who had been inaugurated in 1945. The ups and downs of enrollment associated with World War II and the Korean War were among Mr. House's problems. As the figures in Table 6–1 show, the fluctuations were considerable.

TABLE 6–1

In 1940	student	enrollment	was	4,100
In 1944	"	"	"	1,700
In 1948	"	"	"	7,600
In 1950	"	"	"	6,900
In 1952	"	"	"	5,500
In 1954	"	"	"	6,200
In 1956	"	"	"	7,300

Note: All figures here are rounded to the nearest 100.

Chancellor House's administration had found these fluctuations unpredictable, not surprisingly. As a result, budgeting, financing, and personnel planning were difficult and deficient. In his report for 1952, the Chancellor wrote:

. . . As the veterans finished their work and left, and as Korea and other factors caused our enrollment to decline, and as our appropriations and earned income declined, we had to take advantage of every vacancy caused by death or resignation and commandeer the money vacated to balance our budget. Consequently, some of our departments, as for example, Philosophy, Geology, History,

Physics, have been able to replace professors who died or resigned. And in every department as major and minor men were lost for one reason or another we have been unable to add men to teach the new things that it is our duty to keep up with if we are to do our work.

In his book *The University of North Carolina, 1900–1930: The Making of a Modern University*, Louis R. Wilson, the librarian, traced with praise and pride the development of his state's university. The leadership of "great men"—four presidents (as they were previously called) and selected faculty —attracted Wilson's attention. With the commencement exercises of June 1930, he concluded his book. At that time President Harry W. Chase resigned to go to the University of Illinois, and he and Francis P. Venable (President 1900–14) were awarded honorary doctorates by the University. Wilson wrote:

Thus, upon this notable occasion, the initiator and the completer of the transition with which this record has dealt passed on to their successor the University, full-statured and mature, to lead it through depression, consolidation, war and a troubled peace, into an increasingly significant and distinguished future.[2]

In 1953, twenty-three years later, the president of the Consolidated University, Gordon Gray, an alumnus and former Secretary of the Army, took a different view. He thought his institutions were something less than "full-statured and mature." Organizational changes were necessary, he reported to the Board of Trustees. And the changes were synonymous with bureaucratization.

Gray observed that organizational and administrative changes were required not only by growth itself but also by the conditions of that growth. Previously, the Consolidated University had grown by exploiting opportunities one at a

[2] *The University of North Carolina, 1900–1930.* (Chapel Hill: University of North Carolina Press, 1957), p. 598. A second volume, beginning with 1930, was scheduled for publication in 1964 after our study was completed.

time, and not in line with any master plan. In what he termed "the first era of consolidation," such *ad hoc* developments, flexible and informal arrangements, were appropriate. Dr. Frank P. Graham, his predecessor, had provided these with skill, he said. Now in his own administration in the 1950's he found that "existing organizational arrangements cannot carry the increased load . . . they hinder the educational work of the university."[3] Perhaps anticipating faculty opposition, or maybe expressing some nostalgia of his own, President Gray paused to recognize a "real virtue" in maintaining many of the earlier informal relationships between administrators, faculty, and students.[4] He then proceeded to catalogue the bureaucratic innovations which he was making, and which he said were "confirmed by the judgment of nature."

Changes already made by 1953 included: (1) the office of provost, to co-ordinate educational policies among the three institutions; (2) the office of assistant to the president; (3) the establishment of regular monthly meetings of the chancellors with the president and his staff; (4) an orientational program for the trustees; (5) an emphasis on establishing administrative responsibilities and strength in the offices of chancellors, deans, and department chairmen; and (6) finally an annual All-University Faculty Conference on the state of the University.

Still other administrative innovations were to come out of a management-engineering survey, Gray said.

Perhaps the most far reaching organizational changes will grow out of the survey of all administrative arrangements in the University currently being carried on by the management engineering firm of Cresap, McCormick and Paget. This survey is in its final stages; reports and recommendations will shortly be coming into my office. When completed these reports and recommendations will be

[3] Gordon Gray, The President's Report, 1948–53 (Chapel Hill, 1953), p. 6.
[4] *Ibid.*, p. 7.

131

studied at length. A broad base of faculty advice on them will be sought and carefully considered. Following this, proposed changes and administrative structure will be submitted to the Board of Trustees in accordance with the University Code.[5]

At Chapel Hill the management engineers had their work cut out for them, even if they did no more than chart existing structures of administration. As Figure 6–1 shows, Chancellor House in 1953 had thirty-two officials who were supposed to report to him directly: nine for student affairs; six deans of professional schools, including the administrator of the division of health affairs; six institute directors; four officers responsible for alumni, public-relations, and development activities, together with a dean of the general college, dean of the college of arts and sciences, director of libraries, chairman of the department of statistics, director of the university press, the comptroller and business manager. In addition to these thirty-two officers, the chart shows that Mr. House was expected to deal with six committees, with the president, and of course with the board of trustees on certain matters.

In 1956 the authors found the organizational maze more complex even than Figure 6–1. There were in fact thirty governing boards, twenty-two standing committees of the Faculty Council, and forty *ad hoc* committees created by the Chancellor himself. Of his forty *ad hoc* committees, Chancellor House said, "Most of them keep no minutes. They advise me only informally where they think it necessary. If you want to find out what they do, you had better talk to their chairman."

Quite in keeping with rational organization practices, the management engineers recommended a simpler and tighter administrative structure. Figure 6–2 depicts their proposed organization. Three vice-chancellors were recommended—for academic affairs, student affairs, medical affairs (actually a change in title from "administrator")—plus an assistant for

[5] *Ibid.*

public relations and development. The Chancellor's relation to the Faculty Council and to the six standing committees thereof would remain unchanged under the Cresap, Mc-Cormick, and Paget reorganization. A dean of graduate studies and an administrative assistant to the chancellor would work in his office. The four new positions and the business manager —all at the vice-chancellor level—would have the effect of reducing from thirty-two to five the line officers reporting directly to the Chancellor.

The Cresap, McCormick, and Paget operatives were not strangers to the ways of universities. Their firm was one selected by the Ford Foundation as competent to work on academic-management problems, and North Carolina was not their first university client. They carefully avoided any scrutiny of the internal arrangements of departments, schools, and colleges. They stayed away from the Faculty Council. And they took every opportunity to say that "academic affairs" were not their concern; only "business-management" matters were.

The Faculty Council was the all-university legislative body. It consisted of ninety-one members; thirty-three ex-officio, including the Chancellor and his staff, deans and division chairmen. The fifty-eight members were elected by their respective divisions or schools for three-year terms. The tasks of the Council's twenty-two standing committees ranged from the determination of general policies for consideration by the Council or the Chancellor, to minor administrative work in connection with English composition, regulation of student dances, war credits for veterans, and "The Sullivan Award," for example. Another kind of committee was to be created—a special Committee on Faculty Participation in University Government. But first the reader's attention is directed to other features of the setting in which our succession of chancellors occurred.

Administrative Style

To understand the style of the first chancellor in our succession chronicle, Robert House, one must know something of the office. This office is one of high prestige; perhaps more commanding than many university presidencies in other states. It may, indeed, outrank the Consolidated University presidency in the eyes of many North Carolinians, for it is a much older office, and its occupants have frequently been powerful and revered men in the state. Behind the prestige of the chancellorship (until 1931 "the presidency") are several historic facts about the state.

North Carolina was not a rich plantation state in the antebellum South. Its people in unusual proportion—both Negroes and whites—were yeomen farmers, petty artisans, and tradesmen. Especially was this the case in the west and in the central Piedmont area, where industrialization began early for the South. In this "vale of humility between two mountains of conceit"—as white North Carolinians still like to say of their state when comparing it with South Carolina and Virginia—education was highly valued, and it was to Chapel Hill that they looked for and got educational leadership, especially after 1876.

This leadership was broadly educational; the presidents gave both political and pedagogic leadership to the cause of public schools as well as to higher education and extension services. Also, Chapel Hill faculty and university heads figured prominently in social and economic reforms in the state during the depression of the 1930's. Frank P. Graham, then both president and chancellor, distinguished himself by service on numerous government commissions and boards. Thus, he served not only the people of his state, but also the southern region and the nation.

The influence and penetration of the University at Chapel

134

Hill across the state was no doubt furthered by the board of trustees, having, as it does, one member from each of 100 counties. The people of the state felt close to the University and they looked to it for what was still, in the 1950's, scarce and highly valued services—higher education and educational leadership.

As a result of historic contributions and service to the state, the university leadership is now endowed with a measure of charisma as well as unusual prestige. In the ceremonials of commencements, convocations, and inaugurations, as well as the accouterments (house, servants, car) and symbols (assistants and furnishings), the chancellorship was set apart and its powers magnified. To the public, the occupant of this office was the chief custodian of higher education and, as such, the custodian also of great traditions and much power.

Robert House was "a Tar Heel born and a Tar Heel bred"—to borrow a phrase from a University song. Moreover, he was an avid student of North Carolina history, folklore, and traditions. By age fifty, he had become a patrimonial figure in action and appearance: tall and dignified, relaxed and witty, or stern and serious as occasion demanded.

House was born in an eastern North Carolina country town in 1892. He got his A.B. at Chapel Hill in 1916, and spent the next year at Harvard. He taught public school and worked as a state archivist before returning to Chapel Hill. In 1934 President Graham made him executive secretary of the University. Then, when Mr. Graham went to the Consolidated University presidency full-time in 1945, House was made chancellor of the University at Chapel Hill.

Mr. House looked and acted like a fatherly country squire. He was fond of referring to the University family, and he made it his business to know personally a surprising number of the faculty and students, wives and children, as well as the people of the town and state. He was concerned about their

135

welfare and he wanted them to know it.[6] His country humor and harmonica-playing delighted students and alumni.

Like his predecessor, Frank Graham, Mr. House was a relaxed administrator who sought to keep a happy ship, though he never seemed especially concerned about the course, educational plans, and policies. He read at home in the early mornings. He would arrive at his office around ten and leave at four, when he toured on foot and by car to the gym and playing fields, and to various university affairs in Chapel Hill and around the state. His philosophy of "live and let live" fitted well the designs of both inactive and entrepreneurial chairmen and professors.

In his speeches, Mr. House reminded his audiences of the state's traditions and declared for more and better education. He seemed to enjoy ritual occasions and ceremonial performances. With younger, ambitious, and articulate faculty he was not altogether at ease. His gentle and gentlemanly manner would have been ill-suited to a rationally managed bureaucracy whose dictum was "publish or perish." His book, *Miss Sue and the Sheriff,* revealed his preference for people of quality in a near-Victorian sense. "Who are you?" not "What have you done?" was the critical question.

By 1955, the House administration was almost a gerontocracy, a government by the elders. The deans of the college and the graduate school, as well as many department chairmen, were in their sixties. The great majority were North Carolinians and Southerners: only a few were Yankees. Most of them were many years removed from scholarly writing and research.

Although the style of the House regime—the chancellor and his lieutenants, the older deans and department heads—was

[6] "That the patrimonial ruler sees to the welfare of his subjects is the basis on which he legitimates his rule in his won and in their eyes"— R. Bendix, *Max Weber: An Intellectual Portrait* (New York: Doubleday, 1960), p. 364.

characteristically traditional and patrimonial, it did have bureaucratic qualities. The very fact that the University is a state university—publicly chartered and publicly financed—meant that its ultimate authority was legally and rationally derived. Its very size, differentiation, and complexity necessitated a degree of orderly management of a bureaucratic sort. And this there was, alongside the folksy and informal manner, the traditional authority and patrimonial manner.

The House administration was the kind of social mixture which frequently occurs in periods of transition: between phases of institutional development and group life. But one element was subordinated at the highest levels of decision: collegiality. This was not a collegial administration in which policy (including budget) decisions were made by groups of colleagues meeting as equals. Though a plethora of committees, boards, and informal consultations gave it a representative quality, the House administration seemed less representative of faculty interests as time went by. The faculty became more and more dissatisfied, more and more articulate about their dissatisfaction: they had too little influence on the policies of the University. The particulars of dissatisfaction included a variety of conditions: low salaries, vacancies unfilled, poor communications, professionalism in athletics, and so on. No matter whether real or imagined by objective standards, they were real in their consequences, as we will show. And the implicit assumption was that if the faculty could make itself felt and heard in the administration, these unsatisfactory conditions would be corrected.

Faculty Reaction to the Style

The faculty's dissatisfaction with the House regime, and the need to express it, gave momentum to a variety of social developments both formal and informal, official and unofficial. The protest movement began in 1947 soon after World War II.

Younger faculty had returned from war service. They were joined by new appointees, mostly in the lower ranks and under thirty-five years of age. Government by the elders, however benevolent, was no guarantee that all would be well, they thought. Several small groups of faculty no doubt formed to discuss common scholarly and organizational concerns. One group Demerath knew intimately, for he was a member from its beginning. As it turned out, the group proved to be an agency for change, including much of that reported here, although it was not so intended.

The group to which we refer began meeting one Sunday night a month (October–May) in 1947 and continued until about 1959. There were about twenty-five members from the departments of political science, economics, social work, the medical school, sociology and anthropology, history, and the law school. The conversational fare included events, issues and men in national and international affairs, higher education, the arts, and sports. Conversation was aided by drink and food, the members taking turns as hosts in their own houses.

The most frequent topics were affairs of the University and the state. Salaries, admissions, administrators and their selection, relations between the faculty and the board of trustees, and big-time athletics (particularly football and basketball) were the major subjects. A few years later, desegregation and civil rights became prime subjects. The group organized itself spontaneously and with no special leadership. In retrospect, it seems there were principally two social bases, two common bonds: (1) liberal attitudes toward a set of shared educational and administrative concerns, and (2) mutual respect and pleasure in one another's company.

Eventually, the group came to call itself the Chowder and Marching Society, a name taken from a comic strip. No publicity of any kind was given to the group; only the members and occasional guests seemed to know about it. Plans and agendas were avoided. Nevertheless, several things had their beginnings or got their guidance in the Chowder and Marching Society.

To begin with, the group revived the local chapter of the American Association of University Professors after several years of desuetude during World War II. Of the first five presidents of the chapter after the war, four came from the Chowder and Marching ranks, which also provided other office holders. When Frank Graham was appointed to the Senate in 1949, several members of the group promoted official faculty representation with the Board of Trustees (as co-opted members of a trustees' committee) to select a successor. Concurrently, the AAUP chapter formed its own "president search committee," and then relayed its own panel of names to the committee of trustees and the official faculty representatives, some of whom were Chowder and Marchers.

Six members of the Chowder and Marching Society were to become deans and top officials of the University beginning in 1956. Several informal meetings with trustees, including the chairman of the board, did much to arrange for desegregation in the University after the Supreme Court decision of 1954. The law-school dean and two of his faculty belonged to the group, and this was the first school in the University to desegregate. Other group members served in the Chapel Hill town government as members of the school board and the planning board. One member was chairman of the local school board and was responsible for the desegregation of the public schools in Chapel Hill. Several supported a local minister, one of the early advisers on non-violence techniques, in his battle with the Southern Presbyterian Church. Eventually, secession of the minister and supporters led to a new biracial Community Church in 1953.

The collegial Chowder and Marchers' influence was greatly supplemented by the authority of the official faculty, who had become increasingly concerned over their lack of power. When President Gray chose to plan and reorganize bureaucratically, with the benefit of management engineers, the faculty's anxiety level went up perceptibly. Neither Mr. Gray nor Chancellor House justified the engineers' proposals to the satisfaction of many faculty. They feared a blanket of bureaucracy was about to still what voice they did have. The findings of the Gray Commission (appointed by President Truman, with Gordon Gray as chairman) in the case of Professor Robert Oppenheimer did not lessen their concern. The Faculty Council was a body they could and did use—with support and leadership again from members of the Chowder and Marching Society. In November 1955 the Council voted to create a "Select Committee on Faculty Participation in University Government."

The Council's Select Committee was directed to study faculty participation in policy determinations. (It was as often called the committee on "faculty action.") The circumstances that led to the resolution creating the Committee were set forth in the Committee's report (April 1956) as follows:

In interpreting its mandate, the Committee has been influenced by the circumstances which led to the adoption of this resolution. The background was the Council consideration of the Cresap, McCormick and Paget report on University Management. Numerous questions arose as to the effects of the implementation of this report on the instrument of Faculty Government and the participation of the faculty in the determination of University policy. It was recognized that the changes that were being made were required by the increasing size of the University, which rendered the previous organization for the management of affairs inadequate. Nevertheless, there was concern lest the development of machinery conducive to greater efficiency in administration might reduce faculty participation in the making of important decisions.

The Committee members came from biology, business, chemistry, English, political science, and sociology (Demerath). Professor C. B. Robson, the chairman of political science, was the Committee's chairman. To get the facts on faculty participation, a questionnaire was used, and Taylor—

then a graduate student at Chapel Hill—was the Committee's staff man. The questionnaire worked very well, 63 per cent of the full-time faculty completing it (318 of 506) and constituting a good cross-section, or "representative sample." This survey, in February 1956, gave us the first, or "pre-change" data for what was to become our before-and-after study of succession. Its principal findings are summarized in the rest of this chapter.

The questionnaire covered five main topics. Three of them we elected to treat as *outcome variables*. That is to say, in the scheme for the research and data analysis, these topics were handled as products or results of administration: (1) the general excellence of the University as rated by the faculty; (2) faculty satisfaction with professional and personal conditions; (3) faculty ratings of their influence on educational policies. It was expected that change in administrative style, which was the *independent variable* in the research scheme, would produce changes in the outcome variables. The remainder of this chapter depicts these three variables as they were in February 1956 while Chancellor House was still in office and before he retired one year later. Then, in Chapter 8, we shall observe the same variables for 1960 and compare them with 1956, three years after Chancellor Aycock had taken office.

The two other topics of the Faculty Council's questionnaire were (4) faculty participation in university government, and (5) adequacy of information and communication as rated by the faculty. These topics we have treated as intervening variables, operating between the independent variable of administrative style and the three outcome variables, carrying or reflecting the force of the former on the latter. Data on the intervening variables also serve to describe statistically something of the administrative styles of Chancellors House and Aycock. The independent and intervening variables are dealt with, appropriately enough, in the chapter "intervening" between the 1956 situation and that found in 1960—Chapter 7.

But first let us see, according to the Council's survey, how the faculty rated the Chapel Hill situation in 1956 before the change.

Faculty Views and Attitudes in 1956

The faculty were asked to consider nine aspects of the University's "over-all educational excellence" and rate them in comparison with "other universities you know." There were five possible ratings for each item: very good, good, average, poor, very poor. Two items were rated good and very good more often than not: faculty scholarship, graduate and professional education. Three were rated mainly as average or worse: undergraduate education, public relations, and administration. Table 6–2 puts the nine aspects of general excellence

TABLE 6–2

1956

Mean Scores
Nine Aspects of General Excellence
(lower mean scores = more excellence)

	Rank Order	Mean Score
Faculty scholarship	1	1.98
Graduate and professional education	2	2.08
Intramural athletics	3	2.52
Student government	4	2.56
Extracurricular student life	5	2.67
Inter-collegiate athletics	6	2.78
Undergraduate education	7	2.86
Public relations	8	2.90
Administration	9	3.07
TOTALS	—	2.60

in rank order from most to least excellence, and shows the mean scores for each of the several items. Administration was at the bottom—the worst rated of all items.

After evaluating over-all educational excellence of the University, the faculty were asked, "with reference to your own personal and professional needs, how do you rate these conditions at UNC?" The same alternatives could be checked for these eight items as for the nine preceding: very good, good, average, poor, and very poor. The good and very good responses were more numerous than the poor and very poor. They greatly outnumbered also those marked average.

However, when conditions that are directly affected by university administration are compared with the others (personal enjoyment of life in Chapel Hill, family satisfaction with the community), a sharp difference in response pattern is revealed. As Table 6–3 shows, there is a spread of more than .70 be-

TABLE 6–3

1956

Mean Scores
Seven Professional and Personal Satisfactions
(lower mean scores = more satisfaction)

	Rank Order	Mean Score
Enjoyment of life in Chapel Hill	1	1.66
Family satisfaction with community	2	1.67
Scholarly-achievement requisites	3	2.40
Good-teaching requisites	4	2.58
Present salary	5	3.12
Opportunity for promotion in rank	6	3.12
Opportunity for salary increase	7	3.45
TOTALS	—	2.57

tween the highest satisfaction "town-life" items and the best of the university items, requisites for scholarly achievement. The least satisfactory items (ranked 5, 6, 7) are segregated by the next largest interval; .54 between good teaching requisites and salary.

Of the three outcome variables summarized in this chapter,

faculty influence on educational policies pertained most directly to the nature of the relationships between faculty and administrators. For each of the areas (twelve) of policy formulation *at Chapel Hill* (*italicizing* to emphasize the distinction between the University at Chapel Hill and the other units), the respondents were asked to evaluate present faculty influence, checking one of five alternatives: far too much, too much, about right, too little, far too little. There were so few responses in the extreme "far too" categories that we collapsed them into the too much and too little baskets. The responses in the "too little" column (1,702) considerably outnumbered the "about rights" (1,388). The mean scores and rank order from most satisfaction to least—from least *dis*satisfaction to most is the more accurate wording in this instance—are presented in Table 6–4.

TABLE 6–4

1956

Mean Scores

Ratings of Faculty Influence in Twelve Policy Areas
(lower mean score = more satisfaction)

	Rank Order	Mean Score
Academic appointments	1	3.21
Selection of department chairmen	2	3.40
Academic promotions	3	3.43
Allocation of professional duties	4	3.57
Selection of other administrators	5	3.66
Student discipline	6	3.67
Selection of deans	7	3.71
Public relations	8	3.75
Planning buildings and grounds	9	3.76
Admission policy	10	3.85
Budget-making	11	3.86
Inter-collegiate athletics	12	4.29
TOTALS	—	3.68

In addition to rating the twelve policy areas, the faculty were asked, at another point in the questionnaire:

To what extent do you feel that faculty opinion influenced university-wide decisions concerning broad educational policy? (check one)

The alternatives and response per cents in 1956 were these:

Faculty opinion is:

Decisive	2%
Given substantial weight	24%
Given moderate consideration	41%
Given minor attention	25%
Ignored	3%
No answer	5%

It is noteworthy that no more than 26 per cent thought faculty opinion was given "substantial weight." For most academic men, the administration is bad which attaches no substantial weight to faculty opinion.

Comparing the mean scores for faculty influence and the preceding topics (general excellence of the University and faculty satisfactions), faculty influence was the lowest rated and most criticized. It also bears more directly on the nature of administration than the others. The average mean scores for all items on each topic in 1956 were:

General excellence of the University	2.60
Professional and personal satisfactions	2.57
Faculty influence on policies	3.68

Whereas high dissatisfactions and negative ratings were registered less frequently on excellence and satisfactions, they were the most frequent when it came to influence on policies. This finding reinforces and is compatible with that for "administration" as the lowest rated element in the general excellence of the University (Table 6–2).

The Committee Report and Faculty Council Action

The Select Committee on Faculty Participation in University Government made its report to the Faculty Council in April 1956. Questionnaire results were summarized and it was concluded that the situation called for vigilance on the part of the faculty. It was suggested that this vigilance be expressed in more adequate communication, a more realistic committee structure, and improved Council procedures. The report was adopted unanimously by the Council. The specific recommendations were these, quoted here in detail:

I. *Communication.* The Committee commends the recent establishment of the Faculty Board of Public Relations. The "campus calendar" which is in process of institution at the suggestion of this Board appears to be a step in the right direction . . .

. . . The Committee would like, furthermore, to suggest that a report by the Chancellor of the University of North Carolina at Chapel Hill be prepared and published annually . . . It would provide a vehicle and an opportunity for periodic evaluation of achievements, plans and prospects. It would contribute to the recovery of that sense of coherence and unity which has to some extent been lost in the processes of consolidation and accelerated expansion.

II. *Boards and Committees.* With reference to boards and committees it is recommended

1. that the principles of rotation and wider participation in board and committee service be energetically and systematically applied;
2. that the structure, functions, powers and procedures of boards and committees be periodically reviewed in order to establish and maintain a purposeful convergence between this system of instrumentalities and the actualities of the conduct of University affairs. . . .

III. *Faculty Council.* In order to increase the efficiency of the Faculty Council as a forum for the exchange of ideas and information between the University administration and the faculty and its effectiveness as an instrument of faculty participation in the shaping of policy, the following recommendations are made:

1. that the present Committee on Agenda be developed as an "executive" or "steering" committee . . . it should also exercise supervisory jurisdiction over all the boards and committees that are responsible to the faculty . . .

2. that provision be made for the direction of pertinent questions by members of the faculty to administrative officers to be answered at a subsequent meeting of the Council with an opportunity for general discussion of the issues involved . . .

3. that all committee and other reports to the Council be prepared in mimeographed form for circulation to the members of the faculty generally if that be appropriate.

4. that the rule of obligatory attendance be judiciously but firmly enforced with regard to all elected and *ex officio* members of the Council.

Faculty Participation in Policy Development

The recommendations just offered are concerned primarily with the participation of the members of the faculty in current policy decisions . . . This Committee believes that a faculty that is adequately informed and systematically consulted with reference to current problems and decisions is sure to have the constructive imagination and the opportunity to participate significantly in designing policy for the future. Therefore, it not only hopes but confidently expects that more adequate intramural communication, a more realistic committee structure and improved Council procedures will place the faculty of this University in a position to project its leadership into policy planning for the long-term future.

Such was the situation in 1956. The findings of the Council's survey, and the Council action just noted, confirm the non-statistical observations and course of events described earlier in this chapter. Clearly, the faculty were ready for a change. The traditional authority and patrimonial style with collegiality subordinated that marked the House regime were thought to be unsatisfactory. In the following chapter, the succession and the new administrative style that came about in 1956–57 are considered.

7

Succession and Change in Administrative Style

THIS CHAPTER describes the administrative changes at the University of North Carolina in 1957 in terms of the succession, the successor, and the changed administrative style. We can appreciate changes in style first, in the answers given by faculty members in interviews; second, in a few statistics on faculty participation in university government, and on adequacy of information and communications.

In 1957, when William B. Aycock became the sixteenth head of the University of North Carolina at Chapel Hill, he was forty-two years old. His predecessor, Robert B. House, was the first head in the history of the University to retire from that office at age sixty-five. Table 7–1 presents selected data on the presidents since 1804, data that at the same time tell something of the pattern of succession in the University.

Since the Civil War all but two (Venable of Virginia and Chase of Massachusetts) of the nine heads of the University before Aycock had been native North Carolinians; and both

TABLE 7-1

Selected Data on Administrative Heads
University of North Carolina, Chapel Hill
1804–1964

Name	State of Birth	Inaugural Age	Faculty Member Yes	Faculty Member No	Period of Service	Years Served
Joseph Caldwell	New Jersey	31	X		1804–1812	8
Robert H. Chapman	New Jersey	24		X	1813–1816	3
Joseph Caldwell	New Jersey	43	X		1816–1835	19 (2nd term)
David S. Lowry	N. Carolina	34		X	1835–1868	33
Solomon Pool	N. Carolina	35	X		1868–1874	6
Charles Phillips	(chairman of the faculty)				1875–1876	
Kemp P. Battle	N. Carolina	47	X		1876–1891	15
George T. Winston	N. Carolina	45	X		1891–1896	5
Edwin A. Alderman	N. Carolina	44	X		1896–1900	4
Francis P. Venable	Virginia	38	X		1900–1914	14
Edward K. Graham	N. Carolina	41	X		1914–1918	4
Martin H. Stacy	N. Carolina	36	X		1918–1919	1
Harry W. Chase	Massachusetts	44	X		1919–1930	11
Frank P. Graham	N. Carolina	53	X		1930–1949	19
Robert B. House	N. Carolina	42		X	1945–1957	12
William B. Aycock	N. Carolina	46	X		1957–1964	7
William C. Sharp	Missouri			X	1964–1965	1

of these men had been on the faculty for some time before becoming presidents (Venable for twenty years and Chase for nine). Most of the heads came out of well-established academic disciplines: English, chemistry, history, law, psychology. One was a civil engineer, and his term was the shortest —less than one year—owing to death.

It is hardly surprising that Aycock's successor in 1964 was not a North Carolinian, or even a faculty member. As we will show, the Aycock regime featured more bureaucratic and less patrimonial administration, with the policies formulated in more collegial fashion than had been the case in the House administration. For a man with Sharp's antecedents to have succeeded House would have been quite unlikely, for Sharp was neither a North Carolinian nor a faculty member of the University. Aycock's administration might have been a prologue, historically, to even greater faculty influence, more rationality, and less traditionalism in the future. However, it seems that the outbreak of latter-day McCarthyism, which began in 1964 with the notorious "Speakers-Ban Law," followed by the unusually brief term of Aycock's successor, Chancellor Sharp, might presage a future in which Southern traditionalism, patrimonialism, and provincialism may mark the University's management, at least temporarily.

Succession in the chief office of the University, however, has never been a routine affair. The period of office, likely as not, was apt to be more than ten years, with termination unpredictable. Only Chancellor House vacated at "retirement age," as noted previously. Historically, the procedure has been to have the board of trustees appoint. Since consolidation, the president has appointed chancellors with the approval of the board. The extent to which faculty opinion has been consulted over the years is unknown. In recent years, however, when selecting the two presidents of the Consolidated University (Gray and Friday) and Chancellor Aycock, the board sought faculty advice.

In contrast with the predictions of some sociologists, not one of the heads of the University who are most commonly credited as having been the most significant innovators and educational leaders came from outside the faculty.[1] We refer to Venable, Chase, and Frank P. Graham.

As far as the esteem in which the predecessor, Chancellor House, was held, it is true there was mounting criticism over the minor part thought to be played by the faculty in University government. Nevertheless, Mr. House, as an individual, was highly and warmly regarded by many, particularly among the older faculty who had known him personally and been associated with him for many years in North Carolina affairs. At the same time he was protected from open criticism by his genial personality and long service to the University. At no time, as far as we know, was there any attempt to unseat him or to force his resignation; everyone assumed that he would hold office until he retired in 1957. Pretty much the same attitude applied to his deans; the dean of faculties was fifty-seven years old in 1956, and the dean of the graduate school had retired in 1955 at age sixty-five.

Another important protective factor, however, in offsetting or curbing faculty criticism was probably the appointment of two younger professors (under forty-five) as deans in 1955. In 1955, following the management engineers' recommendations, Mr. House appointed as new dean of the faculty his former dean of arts and sciences. This position was essentially

---

[1] The idea that successions by outsiders are more likely to lead to institutional creativity because they offer opportunities to solve internal problems and better adjustment to the outside environment may be rather gross in application, especially to mixed organizations like universities. See A. W. Gouldner, "Taking Over," *Trans-action*, I (March 1964), 23–7, p. 24. See also R. O. Carlson, "Succession and Performance among School Superintendents," *Administrative Science Quarterly*, 6 (September 1961), 210–26. Carlson differentiates between insiders and outsiders also, and says outsiders have "career-bound" orientations and are "innovators," whereas insiders are "adapters"—ideas not unlike the local-cosmopolitan distinction of Merton and others.

that which the consultants had recommended under the name "vice-chancellor of academic affairs."

Mr. Aycock, the new chancellor, was a professor of law and a native of eastern North Carolina. His family's name was distinguished in North Carolina public education and politics. Aycock got his college degree from North Carolina State and then came to Chapel Hill for an M.A. and Doctor of Jurisprudence. He received the latter degree in 1948, after army service, which he left with the rank of lieutenant colonel, several decorations, and some administrative experience. He was a member of the law-school faculty from 1948 to 1957, when he was made chancellor.

This was the same year in which Aycock's friend and law-school classmate, William Friday, the acting president of the Consolidated University, was made president. Friday, five years younger than Aycock, had climbed the administrative ladder rapidly, but had not been a faculty member. Both men were admirers and protégés of Frank P. Graham, the distinguished president of the University and, later, U.S. Senator from North Carolina.[2]

The New Style Characterized

Shortly after taking office in 1957, Chancellor Aycock appointed three new deans—of the faculty, the graduate school, and the college of arts and sciences. All three were social

---

[2] Students of organizations and management may note that the pages preceding have taken up four aspects of the 1956 situation at the University which are thought to be factors in organizational behavior. They are: (1) the frequency of succession in the life history of the organization; (2) the planning and procedures for succession; (3) the traditions of succession and legitimacy surrounding the phenomenon; and (4) the esteem in which a predecessor and successor are held. See Oscar Grusky, "Corporate Size, Bureaucratization and Managerial Succession," *American Journal of Sociology*, LXVII (November 1961), 261–9; and D. B. Trow, "Executive Succession in Small Companies," *Administrative Science Quarterly*, VI (September 1961), 228–35.

scientists. In 1957 the four men were ages forty (graduate school), forty-two (chancellor), forty-six (arts and sciences), and fifty (dean of faculty). The Chancellor and his deans had been leaders in the local chapter of the American Association of University Professors (two of them were former presidents). All four came directly out of the classroom. Mr. Aycock and two of his deans were also members of the Chowder and Marching Society, described in Chapter 6.

That the new regime would be different there could be no doubt. Between 1957 and 1959 came word from friends in Chapel Hill that budgets were bigger, new faculty were being added, salaries were better, and the Chancellor and his top staff were well regarded by many faculty. At the same time, other features of the University had not changed in any basic respect. The organization, educational programs, and policies of the University remained essentially the same as they had been in 1956, except for somewhat higher standards of admissions and a new program for gifted students in the college or arts and sciences. Faculty salaries were 25 per cent higher than in 1956, but, relative to other universities, they were not greatly improved. The enrollment had increased to about 8,500 and the faculty to 651.

Were there differences in administrative style, in communication, in faculty participation? If there were, then faculty perceptions and attitudes on the matters surveyed for the Faculty Council in 1956 should be measurably improved: that is, more favorable toward the University and its new administration. Could the 1956 questionnaire survey be repeated? To find out what changes had actually occurred in administrative style, and whether a replication of the 1956 survey was indicated, Demerath visited the University in the fall of 1959. There, in addition to conversations at parties and meals, he conducted fifteen formal interviews with professors in nine different units (sociology, political science, botany, physics, medical school, romance languages, dramatic art, epidemiol-

ogy, business school), and six administrators (three department chairmen, two of the four deans, and Chancellor Aycock). After a reminder, or explanation, of the research aims,
each man was asked three principal questions: "What would
you say are the main differences or changes in the Aycock
administration compared with 1956?" "What about the attitude of the faculty?" "What would you say as to the sense of
participation in University affairs?" In the next few pages is a
summary of the results, quoting or paraphrasing interview
materials. University records were also made available to us,
and we have drawn from them as well.

To begin with, the salary picture had been materially improved, to the credit of Aycock, as well as President Friday.

TABLE 7–2

Median Salaries in 1956 and 1960, Per Cent Increase

Rank	Division of Health Affairs			Other Schools and Departments		
	1956	1960	% Increase	1956	1960	% Increase
Deans (twelve-month basis)	13,112	17,500	33	10,000	13,500	35
Professors	11,029	14,000	27	8,204	10,000	22
Associate professors	8,139	9,350	15	6,200	7,900	27
Assistant professors	6,922	7,550	9	5,100	6,600	29
Instructors	5,000	6,000	20	4,100	5,200	27

In 1956 the Faculty Council had found more than 70 per cent
of all larger institutions "above us" in median salaries. Also,
more than 70 per cent of the American Association of Universities members were "above us." Although the University's
salaries were substantially higher in 1960 than they had been
in 1956, the comparative position was about the same, for other
universities had also increased their salaries.

All the people interviewed noted in their various ways the
increased orderliness of administration. An especially sophisticated analysis came from one of the top deans. He said:

Procedures are now emphasized, as they were not before. In fact, substance is occasionally sacrificed for procedure and procedure itself is used to resolve problems every now and then. For example, a man wanted to teach. He is something of a screwball outside the University with a deep and abiding interest in religion. Aycock simply handled it by pointing out in correspondence, replying to the gentleman, that course plans and curricula originated in departments of schools, and therefore he could not consider a request from outside the faculty.

As a rule Aycock consults fully and well. Only rarely does he slip up. For example, in the recent athletic scandals there was a mixup in communication first off between a faculty committee, a students' honor council and the Chancellor's office. The result was that the Chancellor took action in the case which would probably have been different had he had fuller advice.

There were no new schools, divisions, or other major innovations in the structure of the University; but there were numerous modifications of administrative importance. Existing departments were strengthened; chairmen were appointed to five-year terms after careful consultation with department faculty members; headships in perpetuity had been abandoned; deans were now appointed to five-year terms after careful consultation also. Of the twenty-two departments in arts and sciences, for example, twelve had new and younger chairmen in 1960, compared with 1956. Ten new policy boards of the faculty had been established, advisory to the administrators of as many educational and research programs. At the same time the forty-three *ad hoc* chancellor's committees in 1956 had been reduced to only three. And the old Faculty Committee on Athletics, long a target of faculty wit and criticism, was supplanted by an Athletic Council with a policy advisory mandate.

The departments had been strengthened and given a fuller and clearer role in University governance. One chairman said:

The main differences are more order in administration and a sense that decisions are being made. As to the faculty's participation, I don't know about all departments, but in our own and several others I know there is more. I would guess that many people around the University now feel they have a part in University affairs through their department, and on up to general policy decisions at the top level. That is to say, the department is probably a more basic and important unit of University administration and with more participation than before.

The departments were also getting more logistical aid in the form of better office equipment and secretarial help. Of the new business manager, it was said that he figured out how to get what was needed and not how to block requests.

Several interviewees, including "pure" non-administrator professors, said administrative routines and procedures were clarified and emphasized. Procedures by which budgets got made, academic policy issues explored, operating problems analyzed and decided were now spelled out for all to know. Administration was orderly, and the administrators observed regular hours in their offices. One man thought more time on the administrative job was the major difference:

The main difference is just that there are more hours worked. The day now is 8:30 to 5:30 and people show up on time and don't leave early. Before, there was a much more casual approach. Often Mr. House did not arrive at his office until 10:30 or 11:00, then he went home for a two-hour lunch and siesta about 1:00 P.M., and spent only about an hour in the office in the afternoon. Now, with more hours work, more problems are being dealt with and more decisions are being made.

The faculty who were interviewed noted administrative accomplishments with favor. For example, a professor of romance languages said:

Things are more orderly. Decisions are being made. Bill (the Chancellor) is a man of action who doesn't waver. He and the President handled the basketball scandals very well, and the University's policy in this matter is being well received around the State too.

156

Although orderliness and attention to procedures were generally viewed with favor by the interviewees, there were some misgivings. One professor thought that substance was occasionally sacrificed for procedure and expeditious action. Another thought the University missed "educational leadership like Frank Graham gave us"; however, he observed that this, precisely, was what the dean of the graduate school was trying to develop with the guidance of the faculty. The aim was to get fuller, clearer statement of the University's objectives.

An example of the Chancellor's attention to clear line and staff responsibilities was his action, shortly after inauguration, in the area of health affairs. The director of health affairs (the top co-ordinating post for the five professional schools), in his relation to the Chancellor, was being by-passed by the dean of the medical school. At the same time, the dean was in contest with the director of the hospital. The Chancellor moved the director of health affairs up to the Administration Building (away from the health campus), and made the University Hospital subordinate to the medical school. It was now possible for the director of health affairs to co-ordinate the affairs of his division in a way he could not before, and the dean and the hospital director now got along fine, even taking identical positions on most questions. Also:

The Chancellor let the Board of Trustees, particularly those responsible for Health Affairs, know that he was in charge right away.

As the faculty's involvement in day-to-day administrative process increased, the activities of its faculty "watch-dog" agencies decreased. We refer to the local chapter of the American Association of University Professors and, in part of its function, the Faculty Council. The AAUP membership had grown in about the same ratio as the faculty, but there were no big issues, and meetings were said to be less well attended. An AAUP officer said:

Everything is going fine. The administration has about the same aims we in AAUP have, and there have been no real problems. The University is doing about everything it could do.

The Faculty Council was perhaps less important than formerly, and maybe there were more unexcused absences. The meetings were shorter, and followed a prepared and publicized agenda. Committee reports were circulated in advance, quickly reviewed, and accepted with little or no discussion. (These procedures had been recommended by the Council's Select Committee on the basis of the 1956 survey.) At the same time, one professor thought:

There are more contacts, person to person, now between the faculty and administration, due to the fact that the administrators were only recently members of the faculty. They are younger and their ties with the rank and file of the faculty are stronger and more numerous than previously.

The administration, as if to symbolize the value it attached to the faculty, provided a Faculty Club. At the end of World War II the University had inherited from the Navy a handsome Georgian building at the edge of the campus. However, only one large room and kitchen service were used by the faculty together with the public; the rest of the building was turned over to the varsity athletes, most conspicuously the football giants. Later, a small soda bar was built for the students who did not play football, many of whom occupied dormitories nearby. Following the death of the man who, more than any other, was responsible for the "Monogram Club," the administration quietly converted it to a Faculty Club, with a few rooms open to the public.

Another interviewee, who knew the President and the Chancellor well, spoke of their more personal characteristics as these affected their administrative performance:

Aycock is a tough competitor who wants to win in interpersonal relationships. He is a tough minded, highly disciplined, autonomous person. In addition, he has the real advantage of being a secure academician who could get a job in about any law school he wanted, with—to his great credit—good publication and service to the profession of law, as well as to the academic profession.

Bill Friday (the President), on the other hand, never having been a professor, is somewhat less secure academically. He is an other-directed personality. Friday has a highly developed sense of strategy to opposition and trouble. He can smell a problem arising at the other end of the State. He relates extremely well to all kinds of people, and consults fully and carefully all the time. All in all, Friday is fine for the outside job (with legislature, trustees, foundations), and Bill is great for the inside job at Chapel Hill. They're a good team.

Aycock's main weakness is that he is loathe to innovate educationally; is skeptical of cross-disciplinary ventures, new institutes, centers, programs.

Faculty support for the new administration seemed very strong. This was hardly surprising. The top administrators in 1960 were recently in classroom and library. They were young and energetic and were attuned and available to the aspirations and outlooks of the faculty. All had been active in the affairs of the AAUP. The dean of the faculty and the dean of the graduate school had been recent presidents of that organization locally. Even the new business manager had lived next door for several years to a former professor and AAUP president with whom he had been close friends, and he enjoyed many other faculty friends as well. Four of the five top officers and the president of the Consolidated University were original members of the faculty group described in Chapter 6, the Chowder and Marching Society.

In summary, the administrative style of the new regime—according to the interviews—appeared thus, in terms of the four aspects of style noted earlier: (1) In his social interaction, Aycock was an able "competitor" who wanted to succeed in human relations and generally did. He was a sociometric "star" with extensive faculty contacts carefully consulted except in rare instances. (2) He used clear-lined executive authority to define and accomplish tasks in combination with a collegial approach and collegial authority in reaching decisions. (3) Orderliness was emphasized with rules and procedures clarified and systematically followed. Actions were organized by structural definition and effective communication, not by punishment. (4) Aycock's considerable instrumental and social skills—in achieving higher salaries, strengthening departments, and making good appointments—evidently made the faculty more satisfied and more identified with the University. He worked from a collegial base that lent support to his innovations, chiefly in administrative methods and only indirectly in educational affairs *per se*. Aycock, however, was no mere custodian of the *status quo*. His innovations were improved organizational means and a new administrative style, but not new educational programs.

Faculty Participation and Adequacy of Communication

In light of the interviews and University records, it seemed that the succession had brought a change in administrative style and in the intervening variables (i.e., faculty participation and communication). At the same time, the University remained the same institution in other respects that it had been in 1956. But could the changes in style, faculty participation, and communication be measured? What would the perceptions and attitudes of a representative sample of the faculty show in comparison with the fifteen interviews? And could outcome variables (namely, excellence of the University, faculty satisfactions, and faculty influence on educational policies) be measured?

We concluded that these factors could be analyzed, because the 1956 Council survey could be repeated in 1960. The deans and Faculty Council officers agreed to co-operate, and the

Chancellor said we might report the findings without resorting to the all too transparent disguises to which students of organizations are often driven: this need not be a study of the "University of Catalpa," say. The Faculty Council would sponsor the second survey, thereby enabling us to duplicate in 1960 as far as possible the auspices and sponsorship of the earlier survey. Except for the elimination of eight items on faculty influence, the addition of ten "Cosmopolitanism" items, and minor changes in wording appropriate to the passing of time, the 1960 questionnaire of seven pages was identical to that used in 1956. It was arranged to mail the questionnaires to all voting members of the faculty in the spring of 1960, four years after the first survey. The returns were anonymous: 409 (63 per cent) in 1960 compared with 318 (63 per cent) in 1956. All the returns were usable: that is, they were legible. The respondents who failed to answer various items resembled the sample as a whole, and the number of "no answers" was not excessive. The samples in comparison with the faculties are described for both surveys in Appendix B, along with the questionnaire and other details of theory and method.

For the two intervening variables—which directly reflect administrative style—the questionnaire data were expected to show that in 1960, compared with 1956:

1. The faculty reporting no greater participation or confidence in special committees, councils and boards because of the new style's emphasis on departments and schools in policy-making and communication.

2. The faculty perceiving information and communications as being more adequate for the reason just noted, and because these matters were getting more attention.

Survey data on the first expectation have been summarized in Table 7–3. Note that it is University government *outside* the teaching departments that is referred to here: the extra-departmental committees, boards, and councils. The findings confirmed the first idea, but to an unexpected degree: mem-

TABLE 7–3

1956 and 1960

Faculty Participation in University Government
(Excluding Departments)
and Rated Effectiveness of Committees

		Per Cents 1956	Per Cents 1960	Per Cent Change
Member of commitees, boards, councils:				
Number belonging to:				
	0	37	53	+16
	1–2	34	32	− 2
	3–5	15	11	− 4
	6+	5	3	− 2
	no answer	9	1	
Voted in election to:				
Faculty Council				
	Yes	95	79	−16
	No	5	21	+16
Advisory Committee				
	Yes	87	77	−10
	No	13	23	+10
Rating most University committees as:				
	Very important	24	18	− 6
	Fairly important	46	51	+ 5
	Unimportant	18	23	+ 5
	No answer	12	8	
Rating the Faculty Council as:				
	Very effective	14	10	− 4
	Fairly effective	57	55	− 2
	Ineffective	20	21	+ 1
	No answer	9	14	

bership on committees, boards, and councils was 16 per cent
less in 1960 than in 1956. Of the sample, 16 per cent more belonged to none in 1960 than was the case in 1956. This was defi-
nitely less, and not as we expected merely "no greater." Voting
in the election of representatives to the Faculty Council and to

the Advisory Committee in 1960 was also less (by 16 per cent and 10 per cent respectively) than it had been in 1956. Consistent with these findings, the importance of University committees in 1960 was rated lower than in 1956, as was the effectiveness of the Faculty Council.

Survey data summarized in Table 7–4 confirmed the expectation in regard to the perceived adequacy of information and communications throughout the University, except for one item. The "chance to present my views to policy-makers" did not change significantly, according to the statistical test used in the research. (It was significant at less than the .001 level chi square, though this might be an artificiality of the "yes" or "no" response required there.) In any case, the item was so worded that in all probability it meant the expression of one's views directly to the top administrators, rather than through one's department chairman. With departments getting greater emphasis in 1960, and with lines of communication and University government more formalized, the insignificant result on the fourth item of Table 7–4 is not surprising.

Summary

The presence of a different administrative style after 1957, suggested by interviews and University records, was corroborated by survey statistics presented here and in the preceding chapter. Without adopting the reorganization proposed by the management engineers (Figure 6–2), Chancellor Aycock made more formal and orderly the procedures of administration. These procedures were spelled out to all concerned, and they were followed in the every-day matters of personnel, budgeting, communications, and the like. Lines of responsibility and authority, advice and consent, decision and action were simplified, clarified, and reinforced by the very behavior of the Chancellor and his top staff in daily relations with faculty and other administrators.

TABLE 7–4

1956 and 1960

Adequacy of Information and Communications

	Per Cents 1956	Per Cents 1960	Per Cent Change
Gets adequate information on policy problems:			
Yes	58	71	+13
No	36	25	− 9
No answer	6	4	
Flow of information, faculty and administration, is:			
Adequate	4	13	+ 9
Fairly adequate	37	56	+19
Inadequate	50	22	−28
No answer	9	9	
Flow of information, departments and schools, is:			
Adequate	1	7	+ 6
Fairly adequate	34	37	+ 3
Inadequate	55	48	− 7
No answer	10	8	
Chance to present my views to policy-makers:			
Yes	62	68	+ 6
No	30	26	− 4
No answer	8	6	

In these respects there was bureaucratization, but it was *not* the kind of routinization the German sociologist Max Weber described as the anathema of collegiality. This bureaucratization occurred without a proliferation of offices and bureaus, and in a manner that increased and strengthened collegiality. Indeed, the new Chancellor's more orderly, more bureaucratic, but non-routinizing style was a response to faculty demands for greater participation in University government. It was a bureaucratization that derived from collegial plans and sentiments and that, in turn, lent new support and gave greater power to the elemental collegial groups—the departments.

8

The Results of the New Administrative Style

BETWEEN 1956 and 1960 there had been one major change in the University: new men at the top with a different administrative style. The institution otherwise remained essentially the same—in its structure, its educational programs, composition of its faculty and student body, auspices and external relations. Increases of 1,200 students and 145 faculty over four years were not major changes. Nor were better salaries a major change at a time when other universities were also improving their faculty salaries. Therefore, any differences on the outcome variables—faculty influence, general excellence, and satisfactions, all as rated by the faculty—could be attributed to the new administrative style.

Indeed, the new administrative style had four characteristics that led us to expect differences on these outcome variables. That these features of the new style were auspicious ones was indicated by other behavioral research and theory, described in Chapter 2. Although the behavioral studies of executives and professionals had been done in industry and government, it seemed that the Neo-Scientific Management Model should apply as well to academic managers and professors. Underlying, there were the basic concepts of collegial and bureaucratic authority, as set forth also in Chapter 2, which in themselves augured well for the impact of the new administrative style.

The four noteworthy features of the Aycock regime and its administrative style, according to the interview and statistical materials (summarized in Chapter 7), were these:

1.   Known and regularized channels of communication and authority, open and used, between faculty and bureaucratic officials.

2.   Chancellor and team of top deans comparatively youthful, socially skilled former professors whose objectives were those of the faculty, on the whole.

3.   Orderliness of procedures for policy-making and execution, especially through strengthened departments and hard-working officials.

4.   Collegial power facilitated by appropriate bureaucratic authority and process, superseding patrimonial relations and the authority of tradition.

These characteristics plus the theoretical considerations culminated in five hypotheses or expectations which guided the "quasi-experiment." In 1960, compared with 1956:

1.   The faculty will rate their *influence* in policy matters as greater and more adequate.

2.   Comparing *influence* ratings of different policy areas, the nearer (organizationally) the principal control point for such policies is to the academic department and faculty, the higher will be the rating.

3.   The faculty will rate the *general excellence* of the University of North Carolina compared with other institutions higher.

4.   Comparing ratings of different aspects of *general excellence*, the nearer (organizationally) the principal control point for such matters to the academic department and faculty, the higher will be the rating.

5. The faculty will rate more highly their *satisfactions* with professional and personal conditions.

When confronted by the facts, how did these five hypotheses turn out?

Faculty Influence on Educational Policies

More of the faculty in 1960 thought their influence on educational policies was about right: 13 per cent more (Table 8–1). And the difference is statistically significant. (Here and in other connections "significance" means that the tests applied to the differences—chi square and T test—showed that no more than five times in 100 could the difference be attributed to mere chance.)

TABLE 8–1

Change in Faculty Influence, Over-all Ratings

| | Per Cents | | Per Cent Change |
	1956	1960	
About right	44	57	+13
Too little faculty influence	54	41	−13
Too much faculty influence	2	2	0

The change on the first influence question was paralleled by the significant change on another, which asked the respondents how influential is faculty opinion on educational policies generally. In 1960 nearly 20 per cent more thought it was given "substantial weight," or was even decisive (Table 8–2). (Here the probability of chance was no more than one in 1,000.)

Which of the twelve areas of policy did the faculty think they influenced most and least? The mean scores in Table 8–3 give the answers for 1960 and 1956. When the scores are compared for the two years, it is clear that the change generally

TABLE 8–2

Consideration Given Faculty Opinion on Educational Policies Generally

| | Per Cents | | Per Cent |
	1956	1960	Change
Is thought to be:			
Decisive	2	3	+ 1
Given substantial weight	24	42	+18
Given moderate consideration	41	34	− 7
Given minor attention	25	12	−13
Ignored	3	1	− 2
No answer	5	8	+ 3

is in the predicted direction. Only three items did not improve: "Selection of other administrators," "Planning buildings and grounds," and "Student discipline." Everywhere else the 1960 mean scores were lower and the adequacy of influence greater. (These changes were highly significant statistically; in no more than one in 2,000 times could the differences be matters of chance.) Academic promotions showed the most improvement, a finding consistent also with the higher-salary picture and selection of younger chairmen of departments. Faculty influence in connection with inter-collegiate athletics was at the bottom of the list in 1956 and it remained there in 1960.

The faculty's ratings of their influence on the selection of department chairmen, deans, and other administrators are puzzling (Table 8–3). As expected, they thought their influence in 1960 more adequate in the selection of department chairmen and deans than they had before. However, in the case of the ambiguous "other administrators," they were more dissatisfied in 1960. This is made still more puzzling by the fact that, as we shall see in other tables, the respondents thought administration, especially, was improved. How could they rate administration so much better and the selection of "other

TABLE 8–3

Change in Faculty Influence, Mean Scores
for Twelve Policy Areas
(lower mean scores = more adequate)

	In 1956 Mean Score	In 1960 Mean Score	Per Cent Change
Academic appointments	3.21	3.15	−.06
Selection of department chairmen	3.40	3.25	−.15
Academic promotions	3.43	2.97	−.46
Allocation of professional duties	3.57	3.31	−.26
Selection of other administrators	3.66	3.70	+.04
Student discipline	3.67	3.67	same
Selection of deans	3.71	3.53	−.18
Public relations	3.75	3.50	−.25
Planning buildings and grounds	3.76	3.83	+.07
Admissions policy	3.85	3.55	−.30
Budget-making	3.86	3.62	−.24
Inter-collegiate athletics	4.29	3.95	−.34
TOTALS	3.68	3.50	−.18

administrators" worse? Possibly "other administrators" signi-
fied officials in the business and maintenance departments. Or
perhaps they were distinguishing high- and low-level administrators, or full-time and part-time, and down-grading the latter
in either case. That they were thinking of the chancellor and
his top staff is unlikely, for there is too much evidence con-
trariwise. The data of the research permitted no test of these
conjectures. The first hypothesis, nevertheless, was confirmed.

The data summarized in Table 8–3 above showed that
faculty influence varied considerably as between the several
policy areas. And the extent to which influence changed between 1956 and 1960 also varied from one policy area to an-

other. Is there a pattern in these variations? It seems that there is; a kind of collegiality factor seems to be at work. That is to say, the more direct the faculty's access procedurally, and the closer the faculty think they are to the control points in a given policy area, the higher will they rate their influence in that area. Therefore, if policy areas are sorted by their influence scores, one may expect to uncover a pattern of bureaucratic distance or collegial proximity and access. That is, the closer in the organization, laterally or vertically, is the policy matter to the faculty member and to his academic department (i.e., the fewer the non-faculty and extra-department interests in decision), the greater will be the rated faculty influence.

Table 8–4 supports this collegiality hypothesis (the second hypothesis) referring to faculty influence. Faculty appointments, selection of department chairmen, and promotions were matters in which the departments exercised high control in both years. Inter-collegiate athletics, budget-making, and admissions policy were the low-control areas in 1956. In the North Carolina setting, the state legislature, the state budget bureau, the University's alumni, the students, and bureaucratic officials are all potential policy-makers. In 1956 they were dominating varsity athletics, budget-making, and admissions, the low-control areas. Collegial influence was low then, but by 1960 the situation had changed. The majority of the faculty in 1960 no longer saw policy questions of budget and varsity athletics as dominated by others. In greater degree they were now included in the life space of the professor and his department; they had become collegial matters in which the faculty now exercised medium control.

The categorization of the influence areas by mean scores and degree of collegial control, as already noted, confirms the collegial-factor hypothesis. Also, in the movement of policy areas from one category to another between 1956 and 1960, the data are consistent with and lend further support to the

TABLE 8–4

Twelve Policy Areas Ranked by Faculty Influence Scores
and by Degree of Collegial Control
(Based on Table 8–3)

Year	High Control (2.97–3.43)	Medium Control (3.50–3.76)	Low Control (3.83–4.29)
1956	Appointments Selection of department chairmen Promotions	*Allocation of duties Selection of other administrators Student discipline Selection of deans Public relations *Buildings and grounds	*Admissions *Budget-making Inter-collegiate athletics
1960	Promotions Appointments Selection of department chairmen *Allocation of professors' duties	Public relations Selection of deans *Admissions *Budget-making Selection of other administrators Student discipline	*Buildings and grounds Inter-collegiate athletics

* These items changed categories (High-Medium-Low) between 1956 and 1960.

first hypothesis; the changes are in the predicted direction, with one exception—"Buildings and grounds." Just why that area of policy should have moved from a position of medium faculty control in 1956 down to low control in 1960 we do not know. The old buildings-and-grounds committee, watch dogs of a pseudo-Williamsburg colonial architecture, had not been reconstituted by the new administration. And more "Williams-

171

burg excrescences," as one professor said, had been added since 1956. With many faculty preferring modern design, the response here may well represent esthetic criticism and protest.

General Excellence of the University of North Carolina at Chapel Hill

The general excellence of the University compared with others was rated significantly higher by the faculty in 1960. Thus, the third hypothesis is confirmed by the survey data. When the per cents of total responses are compared (Table 8–5), the "poor" and "very poor" ratings are seen to have

TABLE 8–5

North Carolina and Other Universities:
Change in General Excellence, Over-all Ratings
Per Cents of Total Responses and Change

	In 1956	In 1960	Per Cent Change
Very good	13	14	+1
Good	25	40	+5
Average	36	37	+1
Poor	13	8	−5
Very poor	3	1	−2

declined significantly in 1960, whereas the "good" and the "very good" went up.

Looking at the nine aspects of excellence in Table 8–6 below, all but one changed significantly in the predicted direction. Only one item, "Graduate and professional education," moved slightly and unaccountably in the other direction. Nevertheless, it was again rated second highest of the nine aspects in 1960. The entire rank order of the elements (from greatest to least excellence) remained the same in 1960 with

TABLE 8-6

North Carolina and Other Universities
Change in General Excellence, Mean Scores
for Nine Aspects
(lower mean scores = more excellence)

	In 1956 Mean Score	In 1960 Mean Score	Per Cent Change
Faculty scholarship	1.98	1.82	−.16
Graduate and professional education	2.08	2.09	+.01
Intramural athletics	2.52	2.42	−.01
Student government	2.56	2.54	−.02
Extracurricular student life	2.67	2.62	−.05
Inter-collegiate athletics	2.78	2.55	−.23
Undergraduate education	2.86	2.66	−.20
Public relations	2.90	2.69	−.21
Administration	3.07	2.23	−.84
TOTALS	2.60	2.40	−.20

one exception; "Administration," which had improved the most ($-.84$), ranked third from the top in 1960 instead of at the bottom. Not only is the change in this position an important feature of the general-excellence picture; it supports strongly the idea of collegial emphasis in academic management and, more generally, attests to the validity of the Neo-Scientific Management Model in the administration of professionals.

Comparing the aspects of excellence by degree of faculty control in 1956 and 1960, we find evidence supporting another collegial-control hypothesis—the fourth hypothesis (Table 8–7). As one would expect, "Faculty scholarship" and "Graduate and professional education" fall in the high-control and highest-rated positions both years. They were joined in 1960 by "Administration," which moved up from bottom place in

TABLE 8–7

North Carolina and Other Universities
Nine Aspects of General Excellence, Ranked
by Mean Scores
and by Degree of Collegial Control
(Based on Table 8–6)

Year	High Control (1.82–2.23)	Medium Control (2.42–2.69)	Low Control (2.78–3.07)
1956	Faculty scholarship Graduate and professional education	Intramural athletics Student government Extracurricular student life	*Inter-collegiate athletics *Undergraduate education *Public relations *Administration
1960	Faculty scholarship Graduate and professional education *Administration	Intramural athletics Student government *Inter-collegiate athletics Extracurricular student life *Undergraduate education *Public relations	

* These items changed categories (High-Medium-Low) between 1956 and 1960.

the low-control cell to third position in the high-control and highest-rated box.

Of equal interest is the movement of the three other low-control, lowest-rated items in 1956. "Inter-collegiate athletics," "Undergraduate education," and "Public relations" moved into the medium-control cell in 1960. Here again one sees the collegial emphasis of the new administrative style at work, with the result that there were *no* low-control items at all in 1960.

The comparatively low station assigned "Undergraduate

education" warrants comment, inasmuch as the faculty themselves might be thought principally responsible and in high
control here. The reader will recall that student-admissions
policy was an area with which the faculty was highly dissatisfied in both years, though in 1960 they thought the faculty
was more influential than previously (Table 8–3). Is it likely
that the typical respondent believed the faculty were better
teachers than the rating suggests, but that poorly selected
undergraduates were not up to their teachers? In any case,
the faculty's control over the admission and selection of graduate students was in fact much greater.

The strengths and weaknesses perceived by the faculty,
as they rated the several elements of excellence, bear testi-
mony to the fact that the quality of higher education is
infinitely more complex than Daniel Webster's man and boy
on a log. The interactions between faculty members, students,
administrators, institutional traditions, and working conditions
—all in their variegated qualities—are numerous, complicated,
and subtle. To focus on one factor (such as faculty quality)
to the exclusion of others (such as quality of administration)
is to oversimplify and to err.

Satisfactions with Professional and Personal Conditions

Considering now the last of the three outcome variables, the
emphasis shifts from the University as an organization or
institution to more personal and intimate matters. As in 1956,
the respondents in 1960 were asked how satisfied they were
with seven conditions of their own lives. The first two listed
(Table 8–9) are in greater degree matters of non-professional
and family adjustments in the Chapel Hill community. The
last five items, being more dependent on University resources
and more work-related, are mainly professional conditions.

In 1960 larger percentages of the total responses were good
or average; fewer were poor or very poor (Table 8–8). How-

TABLE 8–8

Change in Faculty's Satisfactions, Over-all Ratings
Per Cents of Total Responses

	In 1956	In 1960	Per Cent Change
Very good	22	18	—4
Good	26	34	+8
Average	27	32	+5
Poor	21	14	—7
Very poor	4	2	—2

ever, those who rated their satisfactions "Very good" were 4 per cent less than in 1956. Then, the "Very goods" had been registered chiefly on the non-professional and community items; whereas in 1960, as Table 8–9 reveals, the faculty rated much lower their satisfactions with "Enjoyment of Chapel Hill" and "Family satisfaction with community."

Nevertheless, in both 1956 and 1960 the first two items were clearly more satisfactory than the professional conditions. In 1956 faculty satisfactions (often used as synonymous with

TABLE 8–9

Change in Faculty's Satisfactions, Mean Scores
for Seven Items
(lower mean scores = more satisfaction)

	In 1956	In 1960	Per Cent Change
Enjoyment of Chapel Hill	1.66	1.79	+.13
Family satisfaction with community	1.67	2.06	+.39
Scholarly-achievement requisites	2.40	2.41	+.01
Good-teaching requisites	2.58	2.51	—.07
Present salary	3.12	2.84	—.28
Opportunity for promotion in rank	3.12	2.85	—.27
Opportunity for promotion in salary	3.45	2.97	—.48
TOTALS	2.57	2.49	—.08

"morale") were bolstered by the attractiveness of a quite homogeneous community of about 10,000, which then was only beginning to suburbanize, sprawl, and "citify." By 1960 there had been much fringe construction and suburbanization, sizable growth to about 15,000 in the area, and the coming of many more wealthy and retired people. Also, civil-rights issues were more sharply drawn by 1960 and faculty liberals —a large percentage of the faculty—were now more critical of local race patterns perhaps than before.[1]

Comparing the last five items, the professional conditions, in 1956 and 1960, we find that there was significant change in the predicted direction, except for "Scholarly-achievement requisites," which remained about the same. And the net average change, all seven items considered, was significant in the predicted direction. However, we had not anticipated a contrary change on the non-professional and community items, or no change on "Scholarly-achievement requisites." Thus, we find the fifth hypothesis confirmed on the whole, but with unpredicted outcomes on the non-professional items of satisfaction. The collegiality factor was presumed to be ir-relevant in regard to personal satisfactions. In any case, what-ever bearing it might have, it is probably less than with matters of policy influence and general excellence of the University.

Summary

The story of the succession, and the quasi-experiment with administrative style that it provided, ends with this chapter. Significant changes on all three outcome variables—faculty influence on policies, University excellence, and personal satis-

[1] John Ehle, *The Free Men* (New York: Harper & Row, 1965), analyzing civil-rights activity and resistance in Chapel Hill during the early 1960's, wrote (p. 202): "The faculty was not nearly so actively involved as the students in civil rights matters, but they were a long way from being aloof."

factions—occurred as expected between 1956 and 1960. The new administrative style had demonstrable effect on these matters. And insofar as the outcome variables are regarded as criteria of good university administration, the Aycock regime with its administrative style was a good administration, effective and successful, during the period of the study.

Although a few of the components of each variable did not change as expected, the aggregate changes and the patterns of change were as predicted. The chief surprises were in the area of personal satisfactions, but here the unpredicted movement was on only two out of seven items, and they referred more to community conditions than to the University.

As to the question, "What is the optimum mixture of bureaucratic and collegial elements in university organization?" the North Carolina chronicle provides at least partial answer: bureaucratic channels and procedures used by professor administrants to strengthen and facilitate collegiality. Thus, routinization of behavior and domination by officials can be avoided, and the historic mission of the university may be served.

PART IV

Academic Departments: Power and Reputation

9

Organization of the Departments[1]

MANY PATHS of bureaucratic and collegial power in major universities lead to the academic departments; as noted variously in the preceding chapters on the presidency and on administrative style. And no wonder, for, as the cell is to the body, so is the academic department to the university. It is departments that comprise divisions of humanities, natural sciences, social sciences. It is departments that constitute colleges and the larger professional schools in universities. It is departments—or, more accurately, departmentalism— that occasion the establishment of so many interdependent and interdiscipline agencies—committees, institutes, centers, programs, and projects—as well as new departments.

[1] All three chapters in Part IV are based, mainly, on the Dr. R. Robb Taylor's study *The American University as a Behavioral System: Power Hierarchies in Selected Academic Departments* (University of North Carolina Department of Sociology and Anthropology, 1958; available from University Microfilms, Ann Arbor, Michigan).

Especially frustrating to many educationally dedicated presidents and ambitious deans is the fact that, although important changes seldom originate in departments, they are often blocked there. This is because in most universities, as a rule, departments control the recruitment of faculty, the advice and counseling of students, the criteria and content of teaching, the development and performance of research and services. Here, by the same token, is the "firing line," the ultimate delivery point, at which the university is engaged with its several clienteles—students, parents, alumni, and the other consumers of its knowledge and scholarly services. From such advantageous positions, departments can act to blunt or limit the official powers of trustees and presidents. Thus, as one observer put it,

University government (becomes) a sort of inverted hierarchy . . . Policy could issue from the governing board as directives to be carried out by committees of academics. But the constitution is never worked that way. Instead, business is made to flow in the opposite direction.[2]

Intra-Department Organization

As with most things academic, departments are characterized by their variability. There may be anywhere from twenty to 200 departments in a single university. These may have as many as fifty or as few as one or two faculty. Students, especially graduate students, are sometimes considered as "belonging" to departments. Similarly, typists and secretaries, even charwomen and janitors, may be identified with the departments on whose premises they work: the departmental offices, laboratories, libraries, class and seminar rooms. Though study of all the participants in department life—especially the secre-

[2] Sir Eric Ashby, *Technology and the Academics: An Essay on Universities and the Scientific Revolution* (London: Macmillan, 1958), p. 71.

taries[3]—would reveal much about department behavior in general, it is power behavior and certain related attitudes of faculty members and chairmen to which attention is invited here. Accordingly, when we write of a department, we have in mind the group of faculty who teach, study, or make applications of the subject matter of the department, deliberately putting aside the fact that students, secretaries, research assistants, and others are also involved in daily department life.

The faculty personnel who staff the departments typically are arrayed by rank. Accordingly, they are often divided on issues of importance. First are those with tenure, whose contracts can be terminated by the university only under extreme circumstances—moral turpitude, for example—and then with great difficulty. These are the "full" professors and, as a rule, associate professors. Then come the assistant professors and instructors. There are, of course, exceptions to this system. Sometimes a kind of super-professor appears on the scene, the occupant of a specially endowed chair or "name" professorship. This fortunate fellow usually receives a somewhat higher salary and greater deference than is accorded the full professor. Then too, some departments lack instructors, while in small departments other ranks may not be represented. In addition, there may be readers or lecturers, whose nebulous assimilated ranks are something less than the professor's but more than the assistant professor's.

There may also be teaching assistants or fellows of the department who rank below the instructors. At the very bottom of the rank ladder, they are assigned the most humdrum teaching chores in the largest beginning courses and at the worst hours. These hapless creatures, almost but not quite Ph.D.'s, are typically graduate students in need of money, though

[3] See the astute and amusing comments of Robert B. Macleon, "Confessions of an Ex-Chairman," *Bulletin of the American Association of University Professors*, XL (1954), 424 *ff*.

sometimes it is teaching experience they seek. They are not expected to remain assistants or fellows for long. As a rule they move up and into other institutions. Occasionally they advance within their present departments to instructorships or assistant professorships, on one- to three-year appointments, sometimes with "prospects" stated.

Finally, there is the occasional visiting professor on leave from his home institution. He has been invited by the host institution for a semester, a summer, or a year to fill a temporary vacancy or meet a special need. He may be under consideration as a possible candidate for a permanent appointment, or he may be casting about for a new position elsewhere and utilizing the visiting arrangement as a stop-gap measure.

What about the department chairman, the administrative officer that the uninitiated think is "in charge" here? As a rule, he is a full professor. (We are dealing only with men's colleges here.) In Taylor's sample of thirty departments, chairmen were less than full professors only where there were no full professors present. The chairman, it seems, is expected to be at least the equal in rank of each of his colleagues. Chairmen are selected in numerous ways. Sometimes, especially when a department is to be overhauled or rebuilt, he is appointed unilaterally by the appropriate dean after some consultation with department members. Sometimes he is selected through election by the executive committee of the department, or by those members of the department possessing tenure. In still other institutions, the practice is to conduct an election in which all full-time members of the department may vote. Another practice is for the department to nominate by ballot, with the dean having authority to accept or reject the nominee. And no doubt there are still other procedures, for professors are capable of vast inventiveness when coping with the imposition of bureaucratic authority.

184

As to term of office, in some instances the chairman's term is indefinite: presumably until death, resignation, or retirement. Unilateral appointment by the dean to an indefinite or permanent tenure are the hallmarks of the department headship. The heads are probably fewer now than twenty years ago. Many departments practice rotation, with several senior faculty taking their turn in five-year or three-year terms of office. Or the chairmanship may be vacated every two years, or even annually. There seems to be wide variation as to self-succession in office. One respondent in Taylor's study said that the chairmen in his university were elected by departments every other year, the incumbents being ineligible for immediate re-election. At another university, a chairman said that although there are elections every two or three years, and a chairman is not supposed to succeed himself in office, actually these elections are regarded as votes of confidence, with the same men usually continuing in office. The rationale offered was that the research programs of several departments require tremendous investments in apparatus, and, therefore, there had to be continuity of research emphases if apparatus acquisitions were to be effectively utilized. Such continuities are ensured by minimizing changes in the chairmanships.

Like old soldiers, it seems that former chairmen and one-time scholars turned dean never die. However, they do not fade away—in their power or power aspirations—so quickly as incumbent chairmen might like. Among the thirty departments in Taylor's survey, where ex-chairmen were present, they were almost as powerful as the present chairmen. Similarly, deans are usually included in the departments from which they have ascended to the deanship. And in the few cases we learned about, there was evidence that the deans held more than proportional power in their departments. On the other hand, the deans were rated quite low by their colleagues in terms of contribution to the intellectual climate of their departments. In one case, the dean was in a two-way tie for twenty-second place among twenty-five faculty. In another instance, the dean was in a two-way tie for seventh place among nine men.

With rare exceptions in the smallest departments, there is a stenographer-typist who is known as "the department secretary." The chairman has first call on her services for departmental correspondence. Then, if she has the time, she may help other faculty members duplicate their class materials and examinations, and occasionally do some of their correspondence. She is almost always a social focus, advisor, and information aid for graduate students and the younger faculty. Not an official member of the department she serves, the secretary nevertheless may become highly influential.

Some larger departments also have a faculty member as "secretary" or "assistant to the chairman." These positions entail responsibilities that, presumably, are more than merely clerical, and the power of the incumbents may be considerable. For example, in one department of twenty-five members, the secretary was in third place on the power ladder, following the chairman and another professor who was also a dean. In some departments with numerous graduate students, one may find a "director of graduate studies" and a "director of undergraduate studies." These officers are variously responsible for advice to students on study plans, theses, dissertations. The intent of these offices is to lighten the chairman's administrative burdens. The incumbents may also have considerable power in a number of policy areas.

The structures of academic departments and their decisional processes feature committees as well as positions. Many departments have committees advisory to the chairman, or even with decision-making powers of their own. These are called variously "policy," "executive," "personnel," or "advisory" committees, and usually include senior faculty with tenure, plus some younger men. However, it is the tenure members who shape most matters of importance—such as promotions to tenured positions. Particularly in larger departments, committees are established to deal with specific problems. Thus, one finds library committees, curriculum committees, and publicity committees, to name only a few. These committees undoubtedly were in the thinking of many of Taylor's respondents as they considered the various policy and power questions of his survey. However, data on committees were not systematically collected by Taylor, because he focused on effective patterns of interpersonal power as these operate in the day-to-day life of the academic departments, not on the formal committee-delineated structures.

As academic departments differ in procedures shaping their organizations and chairmanships—selection, terms of office, succession, other offices and factions—so may they differ also in the satisfactions of their faculties.

In the American university, like its German prototype, the uni-discipline department has long been the natural, the indispensable unit. This, precisely, is the structural counterpart of the individual faculty member's preoccupation with his specialty under the presses of graduate education, publication, and other modes of academic achievement. Correspondingly, most professors are loyal first to their department. Such loyalties are compounded variously of allegiances to scholarly pursuits and to political objectives. In any case, presidents and deans have a hard time finding professors whose educational interests transcend their specialties, as Stephens found in his study of the presidency. Accordingly, it is harder for new universities to become institutions than for corporations or government agencies, for example, whose general goals and values may more nearly be enacted and then enforced bureaucratically so as to transcend the particularities of the individual members and their differentiated work. In universities,

also, institutional leaders may be harder to find than custodians[4] or entrepreneurial professors and department empire-
builders.

The power of the single-discipline department as the basic
bureaucratic and collegial unit of university organization is
widely evident. No matter the intellectual inadequacies of
uni-discipline work in many areas of research and teaching,
the uni-discipline department remains the order of the day,
its exceptions rare. Where two disciplines are combined in a
single department, the members are apt to be restive, to say
the least. This is the case even when the scientific identities
of the disciplines overlap as much as do those of contemporary
anthropology and sociology.[5] And it is the case regardless of
considerations of economy or organizational "common sense,"
as most presidents and deans know full well.

The potency of the uni-discipline department is also reflected in the great importance most academicians attach to
membership in the department of their specialty, "their" department. Hence the difficulties of joint appointments, difficulties in the giving no less than in the getting. If academicians are appointed principally to non-specialty posts, they
want membership nonetheless in their specialty departments.
If they are appointed only secondarily outside their departments, of course, they want to combine the best of both
loci, and this makes problems for the secondary department.
There are questions of title, rank, salary, promotion, responsibility for tenure, voting rights, teaching loads, budgeted
position, tables of organization, and others. No wonder uni-

[4] Philip Selznick, *Leadership in Administration* (Evanston, Ill.: Row,
Peterson, 1957).

[5] John W. Bennett has reported the trials and tribulations of several
"combined departments" of sociology and anthropology. See John W.
Bennett and Kurt H. Wolff, "Toward Communication Between Sociology
and Anthropology," in William L. Thomas, Jr. (ed.), *Yearbook of
Anthropology—1955* (New York: Wenner-Gren Foundation, 1955),
pp. 340–6.

versity administrators at all levels are presented with daily administrative problems by virtue of the compelling need of specialists to identify with their kind of uni-discipline departments.

Inter-Departmental Relations

Academic departments are assembled in divisions, schools, and colleges. Thus, each department is given its location in the university's official structure as well as its spatial and ecologic niche: its assigned offices, laboratories, and, frequently, classrooms and other facilities. The ways in which departments and their "specialisms" are assembled or grouped are matters of great educational importance and political relevance. As viewed by the planner and promoter of degree programs and curricula—especially by generalist planners at the top executive level—those groupings are thought best which seem to contribute most clearly and efficiently to the goals of the program or institution. From this vantage point, inter-departmental relations are expected to fit a philosophy or to function positively. Department members, however, may approach questions of departmental location and niche rather differently. And this is apt to be the case also in matters of personnel, budget, and logistics. These differences between department members and administrators, and between departments as well, may reflect the variety of values and beliefs that constitute collegial culture.

As James D. Thompson and his associates have noted in an important theoretical essay with practical implications for university managers,[6] the collegial world of academic special-

[6] James D. Thompson, Robert W. Hawkes, Robert W. Avery, "Truth Strategies and University Organization," mss. of an expanded version of paper read at the 1960 Annual Meeting of the American Sociological Association, New York City, 1960. (Professor Thompson is at Indiana University.)

isms is highly differentiated in its culture. There are differences in values, beliefs, and attitudes in matters of scholarship, knowledge, and truth; and these are at the root of many of the organizational and administrative difficulties that beset the modern university and its officials. These differences are those of "truth strategies"; rules and beliefs about knowledge, about how it is to be sought and sifted; rules that are nowhere more assiduously implemented and rigorously sanctioned than they are in the modern university. It is these differences, say Thompson and his co-authors, that account for much of the intra-university variety of standards and demands in such things as curricula, space, location, pay, promotion, recruitment of personnel, esteem, academic excellence, and the quality of inter-departmental relations.

Four truth strategies have been distinguished by Thompson and his associates, according to the scholar's reliance on sensory experience (high or low) and the kind of reasoning used to analyze and arrange the experience (codified and systematic, or otherwise). In the chart reproduced below (Table 9–1) they have labeled the strategies and classified several disciplines illustratively. The reader will see that no disciplines are associated with the inspirational strategy (IV). Relying neither on demonstrable proof nor formal logic, inspirational truth may come out of a dream or trance, or by revelation. However frequent the "Aha! effect," hunch, and serendipity may be among academicians, seldom are inspirational methods legitimated or institutionalized in the modern university.[7]

Questions of both organizational and spatial location are always arising, it seems, with "the uncertain disciplines," notably the social sciences. Though Thompson puts it in the "direct"-strategy category, another "uncertain discipline," we think, is history, which claims scientific identity here and a humanistic badge there, depending on the historians and the opportunities. Although more and more social scientists have

[7] *Ibid.*, pp. 3–12.

TABLE 9–1
Four Truth Strategies and Some Associated Disciplines

Strategy Name	Reliance on Experience	Type of Reasoning	Some Associated Disciplines
I Scientific	High	Codified	Physics, chemistry, astronomy, physiology, zoology
II Direct	High	Uncodified	Literature, art, music, history
III Analytic	Low	Codified	Mathematics, statistics, symbolic logic
IV Inspirational	Low	Uncodified	

adopted the scientific strategy, especially since 1940, the change has been anything but uniform, even within individual disciplines. And, in anthropology, Thompson *et al.* find the uncertainties crystallized in discrete subdivisions: archeology is direct; physical anthropology is scientific; social or cultural anthropology is a combination. In recent years "the behavioral sciences" claim distinction for an unspecified amalgam of disciplines, as contrasted to "the physical sciences" and "the social sciences." The authors observe:

> . . . the new label suggests that the distinguishing characteristic is the phenomenon studied, i.e., behavior as distinct from society, or political behavior as distinct from political systems, or economic behavior as distinct from economic systems. We believe that the activities of those who claim to be behavioral scientists reflect, instead, a protest against the direct strategy as traditionally employed in the social sciences.[8]

Some administrative problems in connection with the university's professional schools may also be attributed to differences in truth strategies and loyalties thereto. The older professional schools, such as medicine and engineering, draw from scientific disciplines and espouse the scientific strategy as they bring abstract knowledge to bear on empirical or

[8] *Ibid.*, p. 14.

clinical experience. The newer professional schools, whose "professional" claims are often debated, rely principally on the direct strategy. For example, schools of business administration, public administration, education, journalism, and social work schools have usually employed the direct strategy, thereby reflecting an attachment to the humanities and to the more traditional social sciences.[9] These schools have had little use for systematic theory and conceptualized knowledge until recently. Now, formal analytic approaches are being added, such as operations analysis and statistics. And behavioral-science inputs, especially data-collection techniques, are being sought on all sides by the professional schools, old and new alike. Correspondingly, the professional schools are changing in their norms and in their demands in respect to personnel, library materials, laboratories and clinics, extra-university connections, research and service, consultation and practice privileges.

Issues of organizational locus and grouping of the professional schools and the academic disciplines are often related to the truth strategies. Although, superficially, they may seem to be nothing more than "campus politics," the way in which these issues are resolved may have far-reaching consequences for the institution as well as the discipline. For example, in order to avoid the uncertainties of the larger discipline, one school or department may deliberately choose to restrict its efforts to a narrow path of "safe" inquiry and service to another, more certain department or school. Similar restrictions may result inadvertently from a homogeneous faculty. Thus, the very schools or departments that most need new ideas, and new blood, may be the ones least likely to seek them.

Where the social sciences are grouped as junior members of humanistically oriented arts colleges, they tend to emphasize the direct strategy, and any theories they expound are likely to be evaluative. Thompson *et al.* observe that it is in the grad-

[9] *Ibid.*, pp. 14–17.

uate departments of the larger universities, where the humanities in recent years have not been dominant, that the behavioral sciences and the scientific strategy enjoy their greatest vogue. There one finds greater emphasis on non-normative theories, on models and systems, and on the development of precise empirical techniques. In contrast, where sociology is subordinated to social work or to business administration, the direct strategy focused on "problems" seems to predominate. Similarly, where economics is subordinated to business-administration schools, it has focused on problems and has tended to employ the direct strategy of institutional economics. Similar consequences are noted in the cases of psychology's attachments to education, and public administration's to political science—although the discipline, political science, has dominated in the latter case. Where the social sciences have been introduced into technical institutes, however, they have taken on a much more analytic character.[10]

Other groupings are based on long-standing traditions and may not now be important issues, if indeed they ever were. Nevertheless, their educational consequences in the present may be considerable. Thompson and his colleagues remind us of departments of philosophy grouped with the humanities and, therefore, more concerned with value questions than with logic; departments of mathematics grouped with the physical sciences and, therefore, more preoccupied with mathematical systems adaptable mainly to physics and astronomy; and statistics associated with biological or agricultural sciences with little applicability to the social or behavioral sciences.[11]

Finally, in their analysis of truth strategies in collegial culture, the authors note that each strategy has a characteristic way of "going wrong." Scientists tend to fall into theoretical and research routines, which, in turn, exclude possibilities of creative insight by inspiration. The direct disciplines seek to

[10] *Ibid.*, pp. 22–4.
[11] *Ibid.*

ape the sciences for the sake of prestige and financial support, but are apt to miss the substance and make only the sounds. At the same time, the adherents of each strategy frequently believe theirs is the way, the truth, and the light. To avoid or to correct such situations, the academic manager must confront some of the most difficult problems of his craft. On some campuses, the latent hostilities based on differences in truth strategies and related distinctions may be stabilized in a live-and-let-live arrangement, rising to the surface only occasionally. Such a decentralized system may reduce conflict, but it tends to perpetuate the *status quo*. Because maintenance of the *status quo* usually results in departmental obsolescence in fields of learning which are in flux, sooner or later university administrators must take action.

The actions taken by administrators may be directed by the truth strategies they learned originally and practiced as faculty members. However outdated or inappropriate to the decision at hand, the preferred strategy may figure importantly in the administrator's evaluation of such matters as budget proposals or requests for space and facilities. Especially in the case of an uncertain discipline or a new profession, his preference for one strategy over another may lead him to veto faculty appointments or promotions, and may temper his enthusiasm for new institutes, centers, or programs. On the other hand, administrators do not have unlimited power in such matters. They may place two disciplines side by side, but they cannot predict or ensure the nature of the influence or the results.[12]

[12] *Ibid.*, pp. 28–30.

10

*The Structures
of Power and Esteem
in Departments*

WHAT GOES ON down in the academic departments? How do they handle their business? Do the chairmen speak for their colleagues? How can departments be brought around to accept this and not demand that? These are some of the questions that puzzle presidents, deans, chairmen—and professors, too. Answers to these questions presuppose some knowledge of the subjects to which we now turn, the structures of power and esteem in the departments. Taylor's sample survey of thirty departments at Chicago, Northwestern, Indiana, Cornell, and Pennsylvania explored two broad questions whose findings serve as the basis for this chapter: (1) What social forms or patterns do the processes of decision take within the departments? (2) How are esteem and the power of decision distributed between the members of departments?

The fact that divisions of labor characterize all human groups that perform varied and demanding tasks suggests that most decisions made in departments are likely to be made by a few members. Yet, if many departments be the collegial organizations they are supposed to be, one would expect to find broader and more equitable allocations of decisional power in academic departments than in other, more bureaucratized groups. To get at the broad question of decisional power, Taylor asked each of his 211 respondents to rate every name on his department's roster of full-time faculty as to whether that colleague's share of influence was proportional, less than, or more than proportional in each of fourteen areas of departmental policy and action:

1. Faculty appointments	10. Relations with other
2. Curriculum	departments
3. Promotion in rank	11. Selection of department
4. Research support	chairmen
5. Placing students in jobs	12. Assigning graduate
6. Salary increases	assistants
7. Public relations	13. Teaching assignments
8. Recruiting student majors	14. Committee appointments
9. Budget	

The Chairman's Status

With the official authority of office behind them, one would expect the chairmen to be kings of their mountains, at the top of the power ladders. And so they were. In every one of the thirty departments the chairman was rated the most powerful individual. But this was in aggregate, or sum total, for all fourteen areas of policy and action.

The respondents were also asked to designate five areas of the fourteen which they regarded as the most important to department success. With these data, Taylor could then find out where the chairman's power lay—over more important or less important areas. The most important area—so rated by

195 of the 211 respondents—was faculty appointments to the department. Only seventeen of the thirty chairmen were thought to be the most powerful there. In contrast, over the least important area—appointments to department committees—twenty-six chairmen had more power than anybody else. Figure 10–1 shows the number of chairmen in top power-

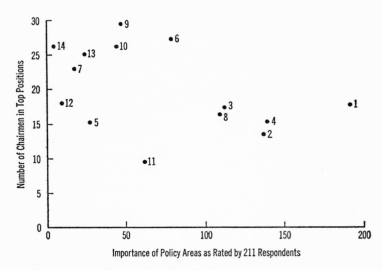

FIGURE 10–1. Number of Chairmen in Top Power-Position for Each of Fourteen Policy Areas (Numbers 1, 2, 3 . . . 14 below).

positions for each of the fourteen policy areas, numbered as they are in the list preceding. It is clear that the more important the area is thought to be to department success, the fewer are the chairmen in the top power-positions. In other words, there is a tendency for chairmen to have greater power over the less important matters of decision. In this respect they are like the storied husbands who "make the big decisions" about China's admission to the U.N., the next U.S. president, and the like, while their wives hold the family purse strings and choose the new car.

In Figure 10–1 three areas appear as exceptions to these generalizations, areas in which both the importance of the policy area and the number of chairmen in first place are low. These are (11) selection of department chairmen, (12) assigning graduate assistants to specific responsibilities or to faculty supervisors, and (5) the placement of students in jobs. In rating their colleagues on (11), many respondents simply did not consider their chairmen to be more than proportionally influential, for two probable reasons: the chairmen are appointed by non-department officials (the dean is the key figure in the official decision); or such decisions are collegial ones in which most, if not all, department members participated. Therefore, (11) is not an item of department policy like the others.

Looking into the matter through his statistical spectacles and eliminating only policy area (11) for the above reasons, Taylor found a correlation of − 57 between importance of policy area and the number of chairmen in first place in the power hierarchy for that policy. (This correlation is significant at the .05 level.) This negative relationship is evidence of the collegial nature of the academic department; that is, power is shared among several individuals, not monopolized by one. The fact that in many departments the decisions are often made by a vote of the faculty is further evidence that these academic departments are mainly collegial groups in which bureaucratic elements are subordinated.

So much for the chairman's status in respect to power. What about esteem? The questionnaire asked the respondents to rate each of their departmental colleagues as to his "contribution to the intellectual climate of the department." As teachers or scholars, how well were individuals thought to be performing their roles? Only three of the thirty chairmen were at the top of their department ladders of esteem—taken as contribution to intellectual climate. Four more chairmen tied for first place with two or three of their colleagues; three were at the bottom or next to the bottom; and slightly more than one-third fell below the median.

The chairman, unquestionably the most powerful individual in the department, is much less dominant when it comes to esteem. There is nothing like a close parallel between the power status and esteem status of the chairmen in most of the departments. Why is this? Maybe the requirements of the job are such that the chairman's opportunity to contribute intellectually to his department is limited. Perhaps his time is too much consumed by administrative problems and routines. Or it may be that chairmen enjoy less esteem intellectually before they are appointed. Policy power may be sought as a compensation. Or those esteemed intellectually may be "saved" from intellectually debilitating administrative assignments. Be that as it may, the fact is that almost two thirds of the chairmen were rated above the median esteem in their departments. Accordingly, it seems that the duties of the chairmanship do not automatically serve to diminish his intellectual contribution, or that low esteem is a common precondition of selection. Future study might attempt to measure the amount and direction of an individual's movement on his department's ladder of esteem before and after assuming the chairmanship.

Characteristics of the Structures of Power and Esteem

So far only straightforward descriptive data have been summarized—the power and esteem ratings from the thirty departments. And principal attention has gone to the status of the chairman. Now let us see what correlation Taylor found between power and esteem ratings, and then note certain characteristics of the structures of power and esteem.

In general, the distribution of power corresponds rather closely to the contributions made by the members to their departments' intellectual climates. The mean correlation was .50, the range .21 to .87. However, it is surprising that in two departments there were small negative correlations (− .07 and − .09) between the two structures.

Taking for each department the ratio of proportional-power ratings to all responses (proportional, less than proportional, more than proportional), Taylor developed scores for the equalitarian character of the thirty power structures. Lower scores meant more equalitarian or more nearly flat structures, and the theoretical range was from zero to unity. The academic departments were not the groups of equals one might suppose. The mean score for all departments was .35, the range .20 to .53.

To what extent were all fourteen policy areas dominated by the same people in the departments? How close did the departments come to having monolithic or monomorphic power: that is, the same or essentially similar power structures in all areas of policy and action? Taylor concluded that his thirty academic departments did display a monolithic tendency with the same persons powerful in all areas, thus resembling the much larger-scale metropolitan structure that Hunter had found.[1] At the same time, the departments displayed a good deal of variety. Some were almost perfectly monolithic, whereas others were quite pluralistic. Even the most pluralistic departments, however, were quite far from having each policy area governed by its own unique power structure.

The people of power in these departments were also people of esteem: that is, those who contributed more than their share to their departments' intellectual climates. However, the department chairmen, clearly the most powerful individuals in their departments, by no means enjoyed the highest esteem.

[1] Floyd Hunter, *Community Power Structure: A Study of Decision Makers* (Chapel Hill: University of North Carolina Press, 1953); also see Robert Prestmas, *Men at the Top: A Study in Community Power* (New York: Oxford University Press, 1964), for references to the literature and report of a study using both decision-making and reputational techniques.

Yet, almost two thirds of them were rated above the median in esteem.

No attention was given to patterns of power and policy-making in less-renowned universities, or in the numerous liberal-arts colleges in the United States. But, as far as these thirty departments are concerned, one sees organizations that, in their structures of power, are probably more monolithic or monomorphic than most task groups or communities, but more pluralistic than bureaucracies. Though there was more monomorphism in the departments than could be expected merely by chance, it was far from complete; and there was also much variation among these departments in the extent of their monomorphic power. The other findings already noted in connection with the chairman's status and the characteristics of the power and esteem structures complement these: they both attest to the essentially collegial nature of the departments.

Although these departments were anything but perfect "communities of equals" that academic departments are sometimes thought to be, their policy and administrative power was quite widely distributed. And there were differences between those matters that were left to the chairman and those that were not. In the thirty departments, the chairman's own domain was typically restricted to matters of lesser importance; more important matters were decided by several department members. In short, the departments, though mixtures of bureaucracy and collegia, were mainly collegial groups.

11

Which Departments Are Better?

TRUSTEES, presidents, and professors who care for their institutions cannot presume a university to be the simple sum of its departments. Departmental practices and planning by themselves scarcely guarantee the future of a university, much less its excellence. But even if it were educationally desirable, not all requests of departments can be met, not all departments can be nurtured equally: a university's resources are limited. Intervention in department affairs, therefore, becomes necessary on occasion. At the same time, it is apt to be seen by the faculty as bureaucratic meddling in academic affairs—always a dangerous charge against any administrator.

Inasmuch as departments are the seats of collegial power, as well as the primary operating units for delivering various educational services, their autonomy is not to be trifled with lightly. When bureaucratic managers must intervene, it had better be for good cause: that is, for long-run gains to the department, or to meet university-wide needs so compelling that the department members will recognize them. As the basis for acceptable interventions, objective reviews of department needs and performance are indicated, although they are seldom carried out. "Which departments are better?" "Which are worse?" And "Why?" These are persistent questions to which responsible university executives must somehow devise answers, though they are usually quite subjective and uncertain answers.

Taylor's survey of thirty departments sampled at Chicago, Cornell, Indiana, Northwestern, and Pennsylvania contained two questions that produced faculty ratings of their departments' scholarly reputations, and of their own personal satisfactions. In these respects Taylor could differentiate between departments that were rated high and low, better and worse. Before considering his major findings, however, let us note something of the problems and possible techniques of measuring academic performance. This will serve to set the stage and background for Taylor's procedure.

Problems and Methods of Evaluation

To evaluate objectively the accomplishment or performance of a complex organization is always difficult. Often it is impossible. In the case of scholarly and scientific enterprises like universities it is especially perplexing. For universities as whole organizations, there seems to be no dependable empirical measure of performance. The evaluative measures used by educational associations, accrediting bodies, and individual authors treat only bits and pieces of a university's facility or its total performance. Separate departments or professional schools have been assessed in terms of selected accomplishments of their individual faculty members or their graduates. There are separate ratings of libraries, laboratories, curricula, operating costs, administrative set-ups, personnel practices, finance, standards of admission and degrees. These partial measures do not produce results that can be combined; they are discrete. Furthermore, they do not measure actual accomplishment in comparison with performance potential, taking into account the resources available to each institution. Nor may any one of these partial measures be applied across the educational board or spectrum. Extension services, undergraduate instruction, graduate education, professional training, scientific research, and humanistic scholarship are inherently different matters for which criteria of excellence must also differ.

So much for some of the present difficulties in measuring the performance of universities, *qua* universities. What about the academic departments of universities? Were the goals of departments more clearly specified, evaluation would be easier. In other words, if the products of academic departments were something other than they are, their performances would be less inscrutable. However, until universities are transformed into routinized industrial-type organizations whose outputs are mere technicians, technical services, patents, or hardware products—like certain development laboratories and trade schools—the products of academic departments will continue to be chiefly mental products encapsulated and carried in human beings and literatures. As three students of a research laboratory put it:

Intangible, unstandardized mental "products" lend themselves to evaluation much less readily than do tangible, standardized physical products. In the former case, evaluation criteria (standards) are difficult to define, performance is difficult to measure, and a comparison of performance with a standard is difficult to make.[1]

[1] Irving R. Weschler, Murray Kahane, and Robert Tannenbaum, *Job Satisfaction, Productivity, and Morale: A Case Study* (Human Relations Research Group, Institute of Industrial Relations Reprint No. 23; Los Angeles: University of California, 1952), p. 2.

In addition to unclear goals and ambiguous output, there are two other characteristics of departments which add to the difficulties and to the organizational importance of evaluation and intervention by officials. First, there is wide variability of inputs—in the qualities, amounts, timing, and ratios of teachers, of students, of financial and other resources that go into the universities and their departments. Second, much of the faculty's work, as scholars and as teachers, cannot be observed; there is low visibility of role performance.

Although the work might be less extensive, the problems in measuring department performance are essentially the same as those surrounding the measurement of university performance. Therefore, analysts like Taylor are forced to consider other phenomena which may be closely related to department performance but which are measurable.

The measurable phenomena believed to be linked with organizational performance have included negative indicators like rates of turn-over among the personnel, and absenteeism. The less of these, the greater is productivity or performance presumed to be. Positive indicators are thought to be "morale" (variously defined as *esprit de corps*, loyalty to the work group, commitment to work goals, motivation to produce, and others) and worker satisfaction, which is sometimes treated as the equivalent of morale. The more of these phenomena, presumably, the greater is the performance.

Both the negative and the positive indicators are indirect. That is, they are not in themselves the outputs for which organizations are designed: they are neither goods nor services that organizations can exchange for resources or "profits." Unfortunately, in view of the considerable effort and ingenuity that have gone into these indirect measures, often they have turned out badly when compared with direct measures of performance, usually industrial productivity. The findings with respect to morale and member satisfaction when related to productivity have frequently been inconsistent, lacking in significance, or virtually impossible to interpret and evaluate.[2]

If indirect measures of productivity are so often invalid, and the productivity of academic departments cannot be measured directly, just how is one to proceed with the pressing questions of departmental evaluation? Can the university official turn to nothing better than bookkeeping statistics, impressions, and personal judgment? Must interventions in department affairs be as subjective in the future as they have been up to now?

One approach to evaluation and comparison might begin with the question, "How good are the department's new appointments?" It is possible, perhaps, to measure the quality of new faculty in terms of their educational and scholarly experience, their college and graduate-school backgrounds.[3] Administrators and professors often attempt this, however haphazardly or unsystematically, when they make remarks like: "Our brilliant new assistant professor who worked under Jones at X University" and "The curious appointment of Jukes to the anatomy department." Just how important it is that a department recruit high-caliber personnel is by no means clear. The most promising recruits may turn out to be "deadwood," while the professor who was "let go" elsewhere may bring luster to his new department. The nurture of academicians in settings that somehow favor creativity seems to be as important as it is confounding. In any case, Taylor's survey of the thirty departments took present personnel as a

[2] B. S. Georgopoulos and A. S. Tannenbaum, "A Study of Organizational Effectiveness," *American Sociological Review,* XXII, 5 (October 1957), 534-5.

[3] The reader is referred to the excellent little volume by Robert H. Knapp and Joseph J. Greenbaum, *The Younger American Scholar: His Collegiate Origins* (Chicago: University of Chicago Press, 1953) for a presentation of methods and findings which would be valuable in any such effort.

206

given, and then inquired as to the departments' reputations and certain organizational factors therein.

What of department reputations and their ratings? There is reason to believe that departments in the major universities can compare their reputations nationally with other departments in the same discipline. Faculty members and even many graduate students know who is who, who is where, and who has just done what. They continuously assess one another's scholarship, and frequently teaching as well. In their evaluations, the groups or subjects of reference are the academic departments and faculty members in a professor's own disciplines, as a rule. In addition to these general observations, there is also some research evidence which suggests that academic departments may dependably and accurately rate themselves. Weschler, Kahane, and Tannenbaum asked everyone in two divisions of a large research laboratory to rate the productivity of their own work group, of their division, and of the whole laboratory. The results were methodologically satisfactory.[4] Pelz satisfactorily used the productivity ratings by members of a basic medical research laboratory, an organization he found to be like a university in many respects.[5] Finally, self-ratings of work groups' effectiveness have proved to be statistically reliable predictors or concomitants of actual productivity in the study of a package-delivery service.[6]

[4] *Job Satisfaction . . .*

[5] Donald C. Pelz, "Some Social Factors Related to Performance in a Research Organization," *Administrative Science Quarterly*, I, 3 (December 1956), 310–25. One of his findings seems to be especially relevant to academic departments. He found the level of individuals' scientific performance (as judged by panels of their peers) related to a number of social factors. In sum, performance was found to be higher (a) where one's close colleagues represent a *variety* of values, experiences, and disciplines; and (b) where supervisors avoid both isolation and domination, and provide frequent stimulation combined with autonomy of action (p. 325).

[6] Georgopoulous and Tannenbaum, *op. cit.*

Department Reputations and Personal Satisfactions

It was with these evaluation problems and considerations in mind that Taylor decided to ask his thirty departments to rate their own excellence in a national context. Although he might have sought judges outside the departments who were well versed and expert in the several disciplines to rate them, this procedure was impossible on practical grounds. Accordingly, Taylor's questionnaire included this question:

How would you rate the national reputation of your department in its own field? 1———Among the top five, 2———Better than average, 3———Average, 4———Below average. (Check one.)

On the same page of the questionnaire there was also an indirect measure of performance: a personal-satisfactions question that asked the department members to consider the items listed below, and to rate each item either *very good, good, average, poor,* or *very poor.*

1. Present salary
2. Opportunity for salary increase
3. Requisites for good teaching
4. Requisites for scholarly achievement
5. Personal enjoyment of the local community
6. Family satisfaction with the local community
7. Social relations with department colleagues
8. Your department as a place to work
9. Morale of your department colleagues

The first six items were taken from the faculty-satisfaction index noted in Chapter 9 in connection with the surveys at the University of North Carolina. Items 7, 8, 9 have been used in numerous surveys of organizational morale and satisfaction.

The thirty departments as a whole rated their reputations slightly better than average. Their mean score was 3.09 on a possible range from 1.00 (below average) to 4.00 (among the top five departments nationally.) The departments' actual self-ratings were from 2.00 up to 4.00, the latter value occurring in two instances and the former in one, as the table of scores in Appendix C shows.

Satisfaction scores, on a possible range from 1.00 (very poor) to 5.00 (very good), actually ran from a low of 3.11 to a high of 4.45. The mean score for Taylor's thirty departments was 3.85, not far from good, which would have been 4.00. Not only was the mean score a high one; so too was the 3.11 low, which was above the rating of average. However, when one considers the stature of the five universities whose departments were sampled (Cornell, Chicago, Indiana, Northwestern, Pennsylvania), and the nature of the satisfactions question, the scores do not seem unreasonable. If one regards the responses to the satisfaction items as objective descriptions of conditions within the departments and their environments, it is likely that these high scores simply reflect conditions superior to those that characterize other less prominent universities. On the other hand, if one chooses to interpret the responses to the satisfaction items as statements of emotional satisfaction or subjective well-being, irrespective of actual conditions, it would appear that the members of these departments are relatively contented in their present circumstances whatever the objective "goodness" of their environments.

So much for the responses and scores on the reputation and satisfaction questions. What about the relationship between department reputation and the faculty members' personal satisfactions? Is there any connection, or is this another case of a supposed indirect measure of performance proving to be no measure? And what are the relationships between reputation, personal satisfactions, and the variables of department organization taken up in Chapter 10: power and esteem, and in addition the size of departments, defined as number of faculty members? On the basis of the paramount importance of collegial elements, particularly in departmental life, Taylor expected statistically significant relations as follows:

1.	Personal satisfactions	+	
2.	Equalitarianism	+	
3.	Power-esteem correlation	+	Department Reputation
4.	Size	nil	
5.	Monomorphism	−	

In other words, he expected a positive and causal relationship between department reputation and the first three variables: personal satisfactions, equalitarianism of power, and the correlation or parallelism of power and esteem. Size would bear no relationship. And monolithic or monomorphic power in the several areas of policy would turn out to be negatively related to reputation.

Taylor analyzed his data for these predicted relationships by means of a statistical method called multiple-regression analysis. This began with the more familiar zero-order correlations among all six of his variables, taken a pair at a time. And these we present as a matrix in Table 11–1.

TABLE 11–1

Intercorrelation Matrix for the Six Variables

	X_1 Satisfactions	X_2 Equalitarianism	X_3 Power-Esteem Correlation	X_4 Size	X_P Monomorphism	X_D Department Reputation
X_1	1.00	.25	.13	−.19	−.14	.53
X_2		1.00	−.11	.03	−.49	.28
X_3			1.00	.29	.24	.27
X_4				1.00	.24	.11
X_P					1.00	.10
X_D						1.00

Of the fifteen zero-order correlations in Table 1, only two are statistically significant at better than the .05 level, but both of these are significant beyond the .01 level: the correlation (.53) between personal satisfactions and department reputation, and the correlation (−.49) between equalitarianism and monomorphism. The correlation .53 between satisfactions and department reputation was the highest of the zero-order correlations. The correlation −.49 between equalitarianism and monomorphism is spurious because, as noted earlier when defining these terms, they are *not* mutually exclusive variables.

Equalitarianism and the correlation of power and esteem structures are both linked about equally with department reputation, .28 for the former and .27 for the latter. Size of department and monomorphism each correlate only negligibly with reputation: .11 for size and .10 for monomorphism. The variable of department size was included partly to give a bench mark against which to evaluate the contribution of the other independent variables to the prediction of department reputation for excellence. But here we see that monomorphism, a variable of special significance for collegial primacy, is no better predictor of excellence than size, and that is negligible.

In the multiple-regression analysis, Taylor found only the satisfactions variable to be a significant factor in accounting for the variance of departmental self-rating. Each of the other variables were ruled insignificant on statistical grounds. Even when all five independent variables were combined in a total regression equation, and adjustments were made for the number of departments and the number of variables, only .29 per cent of the variation in department reputation could be accounted for. And other interrelationships, being minor and non-significant, do not warrant discussion.

In summary, Taylor's survey data support three principal findings in connection with department reputation. First, there is a statistically significant positive connection between the personal satisfactions of faculty members and the reputational ratings they give their departments. Second, smaller positive relationships exist between equalitarianism and reputation, and between the power-esteem correlation and reputation.

Third, positive relationships between departmental size and reputation, and between monolithic (or monomorphic) power and reputation are negligible. In the next and final chapter, the reader will find discussion of some implications of these and other findings for administrators and for students of academic administration.

PART V

Implications

12

The Case for Collegialized Management

Looking at the American university as a managed organization in Chapter 2, we saw that some mixture of bureaucratic and collegial elements is necessary. Neither the faculty nor the officialdom alone can manage a modern university. Such assertions, however, only raise questions like these: For which purposes and to what extent should executive authority and collegial power be segregated or joined? How do "professor-administrants" operate? As to what the optimum combination of bureaucratic and collegial elements might be, we did little more than pose the question in Chapter 2. Now, three studies and ten chapters later, we return to these matters and consider them in the light of the researches the book has summarized. In doing so, we will not recite the results of the foregoing studies. Nor will we call attention to subjects that deserve further inquiry. These will be apparent in ample number to the critical reader. Instead, the more general research findings are identified, together with certain inferences

215

or implications for action by university managers, faculty leaders, and boards of trustees.

The principal implication of the studies is that universities, adapting to societal needs, cannot rely upon bureaucratization of structures; upon more formal organization or upon more line administrators with greater official authority. Obviously, no large enterprise with as many variegated functions as the major university today performs under the omnibus headings of teaching, research, and service can operate effectively without formal structure and line managers adequate to the organization's tasks. At the same time, there are equally compelling reasons today for a complementary social ordering that is designed to make university management more responsive to the needs and interests of academicians. This can be done, our studies show, by means of clear and known procedures for consultation, communication, and decision which serve to make easier and greater the faculty's participation in policy-making. To create and utilize such procedures in a university is to collegialize its management. Inasmuch as these things occur over time and in degree, there is a process, and this process we call collegialization.[1]

University managers themselves should act to collegialize their relationships. Alert faculties should overcome their bureaucraphobic tendencies and help them. Let it be clear, however, that we do not urge collegialization of all management functions. We are referring only to the management of educational or academic activities and, particularly, to goal-setting and policy-making for teaching, research, and service. The business affairs of major universities are best conducted by qualified business officers who are accountable to the presi-

---

[1] For the term "collegialized management," the reader's forbearance is begged and apology is offered. The term will not be found in the dictionary, but we wanted a way of saying more handily *what* was joined in the mixed management to which the book has referred: that is, collegial and bureaucratic elements. "Collegialize" is the process, and "collegial" is the state.

dent. Business policies need not be made with faculty advisors so long as the policies are consistent with the overriding educational goals and policies of the university.

Nor do we say that professors, either individually or in committees, should perform executive tasks. Faculty participation in university management should be confined to matters of policy, with rare exceptions. While the executive actions of administrative officers need to be reviewed regularly by the faculty and by top managers, very rarely should a professor act as an executive unless he has taken an executive appointment. The more able secretaries, clerks, or minor officials in universities could more appropriately perform most of the executive chores that are done now by many academicians in connection with admissions, research administration, student personnel, degree routines, campus facilities, and many other subjects.

That so many professors get preoccupied with university committee chores is not evidence of collegialization. On the contrary, it reflects a lack of sophistication in such matters. More likely than not, the professors who take on executive chores do so because they seek them. They are "committee prone," even though they may complain loudly of their heavy burdens. Or, the chore-bound professor may have been asked to do this and that by other professors to whom he could not say no, and who, however distinguished they might be as scholars, were incompetent committee chairmen and work planners. Within the academic departments also, professors should avoid executive tasks, though with more frequent exceptions to the rule in view of the scholarly judgments in personnel, curriculum, budget and professional work decisions that are so desirable there. As reported in Chapter 10, the departments of better universities are collegial domains in which power is quite widely shared, and the chairman seldom acts on his own.

Problems at the Top

Few universities can go much further with collegialization than their presidents want to go. How far is that likely to be, and why? Stephens' study[2] is pertinent. Indeed, one may conclude from his research that of all top executives, university and non-university, perhaps none stand to gain more by collegialization than the university presidents. Stephens found the presidential office characterized by excessively diverse role expectations and limited executive resources. Not only does the office entail diverse roles; each of the five general roles (Money Man, Academic Manager, Father Figure, Public-Relations Man, and Educator) also demands a varied repertory of skills and actions. In any one role the president may be expected to act as disciplinarian, planner, co-worker, public speaker, writer, analyst, persuader, expert, friend, and manipulator of power. Incompatibilities, conflicts, and frustrations are inevitable. Although it may not be an "impossible office," as one president concluded, it contains numerous impossibilities: if the president meets some expectations and performs some roles, there will be others he cannot perform.[3]

Stephens found that most presidents agree that their jobs impose heavy strains on their health. Ordinarily, they must do much work with relatively little sleep. Often they must attend to a number of matters simultaneously. Most presidents report that they talk with and listen to an almost constant stream of people of all ages and backgrounds: some with protests, some with requests, some with ideas to promote or ideals to protect, some with axes to grind. It seems to be the exceptional man who has enough time—time to make decisions, to read, to

[2] Richard W. Stephens, *The Academic Administrator: The Role of the University President* (University of North Carolina, Ph.D. dissertation, 1956).

[3] Henry M. Wriston, "Looking at the College Presidency in Retrospect," *Association of American Colleges Bulletin*, XLI (December 1955), 504–18.

write, to think, and, least of all, to loaf or to enjoy the conversation of friends in the privacy of his own house.

Many presidents complain of the depression that comes from the overwhelming work always ahead of them, and of the lack of resources to do the work. There are moments of almost complete dissatisfaction with one's work. Rarely is the president able to finish a job he has begun. He must watch many of his most cherished plans drag out year by year or fall short of accomplishment. Almost the first thing he learns is that a list must be made of the things that seem almost impossible to accomplish. This list will include most of the things he was determined to do something epoch-making about—no later than the first year after taking office.

The emotional well-being and self-confidence of university presidents are frequently under attack. Trustees disgruntled over finances, faculty members opposing educational changes or embittered over promotions and salaries, alumni enraged at poor showings in intercollegiate sports events, editors and publishers seeking causes, students aroused by unpopular disciplinary measures, citizens scandalized by free-thinking professors—all direct their bolts at the president. An indiscreet statement by the president or a refusal to recognize the appeal or accusation of the most unwarranted critic may easily set off a tempest. Such criticism not uncommonly continues over years, multiplying in scope and intensity until the president is forced into open conflict. Stephens concluded that such cumulative criticisms probably account for more presidential resignations and dismissals than any other factor. George D. Stoddard, former president of the University of Illinois, for example, was dismissed on the basis of fourteen specific "controversies," among which were listed: defending "pink" professors (a running conflict with several legislators), refusal to honor a contract bill (a quarrel with a state senator), saying things "hostile to religion" (a criticism of a minister on the board of regents), allowing the university radio to represent public questions unfairly (an intermittent argument with a downstate representative), and too many trips abroad with UNESCO (a conflict with the board chairman).

In coping with criticisms and conflicts, the president is often hampered and isolated. First, he is often inadequately protected by the board of trustees. While the board has the authority to settle irrevocably most questions of finance, official organization, and staffing, it hesitates to intrude into other affairs, especially educational matters. The president is usually expected to keep the lid on, to avert or resolve conflicts himself. The presidency does not lend itself to compromise in a conflict of educational ideas. As formulator of the grand plan and visionary of ultimate objectives and purposes, the president satisfies no one by recognizing the arguments of both sides. Is he not infallible and impeccable? Is his educational philosophy so muddled that he cannot act with decisiveness? The answer to both questions commonly is that he is not, and he cannot. He no longer teaches, his scholarly ability has been lost, his own educational ideas are perforce second hand and dulled by the concrete world of action in which he must live and think. Too often in the face of faculty dissension he is regarded as neither leader, co-worker, employer, nor friend.

Through it all, the president, like many other chief executives, is expendable and he knows it. The trustees have employed him and they can get rid of him. He may be sacrificed to save embarrassment to others. His own virtues may be his undoing. He may be too honest to be tactful, too idealistic to stoop to the level of the alumni, or too proud to engage in political maneuvering—either within or outside the organization. He may come to fear dismissal, with its publicity and punishment. All in all, the president often becomes a very tired man, even a sick man.

In attempting to cope with their difficulties, presidents may adopt mechanisms of personal behavior which have the effect of removing them from the social realities of their jobs and their universities. Stephens identified three such mechanisms: isolation, platitudes and prevarication, inertia and excessive busyness. Part of the president's isolation, of course, is forced on him by his position and its associated style of life. Much of his contact with faculty members and students is, by necessity, indirect and impersonal. Moreover, there are too many meetings to attend, too many trips to make, and too many conferences to be held for the president to maintain intimate campus relationships. Besides, as a bureaucratic official, the faculty expects him to stand aloof and not pry into the classroom.

There is little doubt, however, that a more or less permanent state of isolation may be largely self-imposed. The presidency demands impartiality and impersonality, and isolation is often a way to achieve these. Then, the president's faculty relations become cold, distant, formal. He cultivates a cordial aloofness. His use of first names in addressing subordinate officers or professors becomes a bestowal of grace rather than an acceptance of intimacy. It is rarely reciprocated.

Unfortunately, it is almost impossible for many presidents to stop talking. Hence, the description of the university president as "a peripatetic phonograph." Ordinarily, he delivers a tremendous number and variety of public addresses each year. In addition, his diverse roles engage him in a more or less continuous process of private interpretation, explanation, persuasion, or defense of policies and decisions for the benefit of one group or another. In trying to maintain cordial relations with groups of varied views on any given issue, the president soon discovers the efficacy of platitudes and prevarication. Useful are words like "excellence," "growth," "dialogue," "academic freedom" for the faculty; strong injunction in favor of "morality," "sober judgment," and "responsibility" for the benefit of the trustees; "spirit," "vitality," and "loyalty" for the alumni, and so forth. Presidential addresses and pronouncements tend to give the momentary illusion of contrasting colors and a flaming zeal—especially when delivered with firm conviction—but frequently the issues involved come out a dull gray. Such equivocations have earned for the president the reputation for guile and hypocrisy which he shares with the politician and vote-getter. Indeed, he may appear as one wag described him: "A pillar of brass by day and a cloud of gas by night." Nicholas Murray Butler answered his accusers simply by admitting his deceptions and stating that it is impossible for large university presidents to be truthful.

A third possible coping mechanism is that of inertia and excessive busyness. Because there are so many people to see, so many reports to read and prepare, so many speeches to be made, so many meetings to be attended, and so many letters to be answered, all of which may easily be regarded as vital to the welfare of the organization, the president may come to avoid conflicts by burying himself in routine and, in effect, doing nothing. In this case he makes as few decisions as possible, or bases his decisions on generalized rules established on the advice of others—the board of trustees, faculty committees, and so forth. So may the president be relieved of excessive personal criticism. It becomes more difficult for subordinates to discover who personally inaugurated a change or vetoed a proposal. The president is elevated above such petty matters. And there are so many important things that seem to engage him, he cannot be held personally accountable for a failure or an injustice in only one.

Treatment One: More Official Bureaucracy

The difficulties of the presidential office, together with the increased size and complexity of the universities, have evoked different management correctives. A frequent corrective, attractively direct and tidy, is to increase the number of officials and thereby extend or strengthen official or line authority. This multiplication of subordinate administrative offices and agencies—deans and committees, vice-presidents, provosts, managers, chancellors, vice-presidents, provosts, managers, chancellors, vice-chancellors, directors, deputies, assistant administrators, and administrative assistants—is bureaucratization in its classic form. This is bureaucratization as it has occurred historically: legalistic, formal, and authoritative. In this form also, bureaucratization goes on in major universities, promulgated and ordered by trustees, presidents, and consulting firms as they confront the management problems of universities in a technologically advanced society. But it goes on not without resistance and frictions.

More official bureaucracy entails organizational change, and, as with most organizational changes, it is easier to make the blueprints than to bring about altered behavior. For one thing, the traditions of the presidential office itself may be a source of friction and resistance. The presidency tends to be so perceived that responsibilities cannot easily be shared with other positions. Unlike the occupants of many high public offices, university presidents seldom share responsibility with their boards, which are, in effect, legislative or policy-making bodies. Nor do they share official responsibility and authority through clear assignments and delegations to subordinate divisions and positions, as in most business and government organizations.

Although many, perhaps most, critics of the university presidency urge that primacy be given the role we call academic general manager, several other roles or role behaviors that are most in conflict with it are difficult to reallocate or delegate. For example, public-relations man—public speaker, ritual head, greeter of dignitaries, and the like—this role is not easily transferred. As the chief representative of the university, it is the president that is wanted, for lesser figures bestow less status and importance. In this connection, there is the story about the president who got an invitation to speak before a women's club. The invitation then went on to say, "If you as President cannot come, please send us at least a Dean, for we would not want anyone lower than a Dean." The narrator commented, "They seem to overlook the fact that there *is* no one lower than a Dean." It is the headman also to whom the alumni, legislators, and the public direct their appeals and criticisms, and it is to him that they want to speak. Reallocate management of finance and budget? Perhaps, but the separation of these roles in the past has led to conflict between administrative officers, and with the faculty, as well as to subversion of presidential relations with the board. Reallocate the president's outside role as the chief educator and scholar? He is already criticized probably for neglecting these matters. Besides, he is usually reluctant to abandon his own claim to educational leadership.

Moreover, from previous regimes the president frequently inherits officers in subordinate positions who are habituated to their work roles and who may not want them changed. The difficulties in separating certain activities or transferring roles that have always been the president's are not lessened by these legacies. The holdovers are not the president's trusted lieutenants, and personality clashes are often unavoidable. When a board of trustees decides that a particular role is to get top priority, and selects a president with this understanding, the other presidential roles may more easily be delegated or transferred. Under such conditions, however, the changes in presidential activities may be short-lived and frequent. Universities that select presidents on the basis of current priorities tend to go through a cycle of presidents: one incumbent succeeding another as the trustees identify successively dominant roles. Thus, it has been said, there are as many varieties of university presidents as there are tulips, each revealing his true marking in season.

Another major source of resistance to more official bureaucratization lies in certain academic traditions that originated in the medieval collegium, but that persist in the modern university as necessary bulwarks of the academician's position.

First, there is the conviction held by many, if not by most, professors that the university has but one objective and exists for but one purpose: the discovery and dissemination of knowledge.[4] Because the university exists for this purpose, the only legitimate aim of administrators is to provide those resources and conditions necessary for the faculty to accomplish the prime purpose. According to this view, the president and any other administrator should be, not leaders and policy-makers, but servants of the faculty. Then there is the academician's image of himself as a professional person and not a bureaucratic employee. He has mastered a specialized field of knowledge, and by virtue of his degrees and performance he has been licensed to practice the techniques of his specialty. He is obliged constantly to exercise his independent judgment and assume a large measure of individual responsibility. To protect standards of excellence, he is committed as a professional. Very little of his work is capable of routinization. There is a considerable element of what can be called art involved. To advance his profession and add to his own expertise are obligations of great importance.

The attitude of many faculty members today—especially those categorized by sociologists as itinerants or cosmopolitans, as opposed to the homeguards or locals—is essentially the same as that expressed in 1918 by Thorstein Veblen. Accordingly, the university is properly a seminary of higher learning, but creative thought is fettered by an administrative standardization in which most things are measured in terms of practical results by boards and officials who are either businessmen or who think like them.[5] Faculty members too often see themselves as workers in a degree factory, catering to the needs and tastes of the average and below average. They are

[4] Logan Wilson, *The Academic Man* (New York: Oxford University Press, 1942), p. 21.

[5] Thorstein Veblen, *The Higher Learning in America* (New York: Huebach and Company, 1918).

denied the opportunity to contribute to important policy decisions, particularly in finance and budgeting. But they are expected to comply with multitudinous rules and regulations and to standardize their activities with machine-like super-efficiency—so they think. They feel themselves overwhelmed with reports, questionnaires, schedules, data sheets, and the paraphernalia of big business. For the most part their meetings as a legislative or advisory body are restricted to laborious discussion and interpretation of these petty matters.

Ordinarily, the president is neither a trained executive nor an astute politician before entering his office. He must develop these roles as he goes along, or go under. No wonder an occasional president regards the faculty's resistance to detailed orders and directions as a deliberate and mischievous attempt to confuse professional freedom with organizational irresponsibility and license. It is observed that professors frequently violate the very rules they admit are necessary to the operation of a large university and which they, for the most part, establish themselves. They object to coming early for registration, to compulsory roll calls in classes, and to smoking regulations. They will not report grades on time, or give examinations when they are scheduled, or serve on committees, or take their student-advisory roles seriously, or place their textbook orders. They fail to attend university ceremonies and exercises, and they avoid most faculty and student social gatherings.

Few university administrators are inclined to accept the faculty view that the administrator's principal role is servant to a community of scholars preparing future scholars or pursuing knowledge for its own sake. And given the scholars' antipathy for managers and managerial efficiency in the university, it is not surprising that they oppose more bureaucratization or that presidents are most frequently replaced because they do not have the confidence of the faculty, or because they do not measure up to the board's expectations.

Without denying or down-grading the importance of organizational forms that are adequate to the university's functions, it seems reasonable to conclude that reorganization that entails mainly more offices and more line officers is not likely to be an effective prescription for the problem of the presidency and academic management. Nor is it likely to produce an optimum union of bureaucracy and collegium. There are apt to be so many resistances and so much opposition in the presidency and in the existing officialdom, as well as in the faculty, that the therapy will only worsen the illness.

Treatment Two: More Collegialized Management

Can bureaucracy in any form combine managerial and collegial elements in a way that will serve the interests of academic and professional people and at the same time satisfy the imperatives of complex instrumental organizations? The idea of a deliberate combination of collegial and bureaucratic power gets no support from earlier sociological theories. There one finds no likelihood of bureaucratic authority contributing to a revitalization of collegial groups, or of bureaucratic officials seeking to augment or draw upon collegial power. On the contrary, bureaucratic and collegial patterns were thought to be in opposition. Max Weber stated that bureaucratic authority in large-scale organizations always weakened collegiality as an effective control, and, believing that extensions of bureaucratic authority make for organizational efficiency, whereas collegiality reduces efficiency, Weber thought the latter would continue to lose out in the modern world.[6] Talcott Parsons has also put bureaucratic authority and professional control in opposition: the former being associated with offices arranged in hierarchical organizations, the latter with a group of professional colleagues equally and independently respon-

[6] Max Weber, *The Theory of Social and Economic Organization,* A. M. Henderson and Talcott Parsons (eds.) (New York: Oxford University Press, 1947), pp. 400–2.

sible for exercising his judgment in his own area of competence.[7]

The idea that bureaucracy is inherently and inevitably in conflict with colleague or professional control has been reinforced by the findings of numerous human relations and organization experts, most of whom are also professors when they are not engaged as consultants or researchers to government and business. Official authority, hierarchy, impersonality, formality, and even promotions based on achievement have been proscribed by these new experts. Their jeremiads are sweeping, as for example:

In general, organizations built (implicitly or explicitly) along these lines are said not only to discourage innovativeness but to suffer a wide number of other evils as well: inhibition of personal growth and development, the encouragement of "groupthink," inadequate conflict resolution, under-use of resources, and inability to cope with changing conditions.[8]

Bureaucracies and bureaucratization, they suggest, are uniformly negative factors in teaching, learning, and creativity. For the "health" of organizations and for the realization of individual capacities, human-relations enthusiasts urge us to abandon bureaucracy and take up their alternatives.[9]

Such extreme views of bureaucracy are belied by the changes observed at the University of North Carolina. There we saw bureaucratization of a kind that had positive effects on academic life; that significantly improved faculty influence on educational policies, the general excellence of the University,

[7] *Ibid.*, "Introduction," pp. 58–60.

[8] Matthew B. Miles, "Education and Innovation: The Organization as Context," *mimeographed* (Teachers College, Columbia University, 1964), p. 4.

[9] *Ibid.;* Chris Argyris, *Integrating the Individual and the Organization* (New York: Wiley, 1964); Harold J. Leavitt (ed.), *Readings in Managerial Psychology* (Chicago: University of Chicago Press, 1964), especially Leavitt's own piece, "Unhuman Organizations," pp. 542–66; E. Litwak, "Models of Bureaucracy Which Permit Conflict," *American Journal of Sociology*, LXVII (1961), 177–84.

and the satisfactions of the faculty. The North Carolina study gives evidence, not only that presidents can be powerful—a fact about which there is little debate anyway—but also that official authority can be used to strengthen collegial or professional power and, by combining bureaucratic and collegial powers, can improve the academic life and quality of the institution.

What the new Chancellor at Chapel Hill did and what he did not do are equally instructive. In the first place, he refused to adopt a management engineers' reorganization scheme that called for the creation of numerous vice-chancellors. By rejecting the engineers' scheme, the Chancellor allayed faculty fears of brass walls and red tape. But he could not accept things as they were so long as thirty-two people were expected to report to him, and administrative relations were exceedingly permissive and informal.

Only a few changes were made in the bureaucratic structure. The Chancellor created only one new office, the "dean of faculties," though he eliminated numerous *ad hoc* committees. Greater changes were made in the processes and procedures of day-to-day management. These were made more orderly and more formal, not by edict, but by the Chancellor's own orderliness in the everyday business of personnel, budgeting, reporting, handling meetings, and communications. Lines of responsibility and authority, advise and consent, decision and action were simplified, clarified, and reinforced by the daily behavior of the Chancellor and top officials in their relations with other administrators and with faculty. In these matters of process and procedure, changed as they were by officials in action and sanctioned by the authority of their offices, there was bureaucratization. But it was not the kind of routinization and formalization that Max Weber years ago accurately described as the anathema of collegiality.

The fact was that the bureaucratization was a creative response to collegial needs. The new Chancellor's more orderly, more bureaucratic, but non-routinizing style was a response to faculty demands for greater participation in University government. It was a bureaucratization that suited collegial plans and sentiments and, in turn, lent new support and power to the elemental collegial groups—the academic departments of the University. In sum, the four major features of the new regime's administrative style were these:

1. Known and regularized channels of communication and authority, open and used, between faculty and officials.

2. Chancellor and team of top deans composed of comparatively youthful, socially skilled former professors whose objectives were those of the faculty, on the whole—"professor administrants," to use a term.

3. Orderliness of procedures for policy-making and execution, especially through strengthened departments and hard-working officials.

4. Collegial power facilitated by appropriate bureaucratic authority and process, superseding patrimonial relations and the authority of tradition.

Furthermore, the bureaucratization and the new administrative style were consistent with our theoretical model of Neo-Scientific Management, based on some recent organizational and behavioral research that emphasizes the combination of collegial and bureaucratic elements. This theory led us to the hypotheses stated in Chapter 8, all five of which were sustained by the outcomes of the succession, comparing data for 1956 and 1960.

However significant and instructive the new administrative style and the collegialized management in the North Carolina "experiment" may be, the favorable situation in which these developments occurred should not go unnoticed. As Chapter 6 clearly revealed, 1956–57 was a time for change at Chapel Hill. That the succession itself unfolded with goodwill and co-operation is also clear. The predecessor retired gracefully, quietly supporting and not interfering with the new regime. The "old lieutenants" either resigned promptly or co-operated willingly. Their replacements came directly from the faculty, as did the new Chancellor, whom they knew well.[10] The new administration shared the general expectations and goals of the most powerful elements of both the University's faculty and its board of trustees, between which there had been communication and joint consideration of top personnel problems.[11]

An especially important feature of the UNC situation was that the administrative apparatus, as used by the new regime, could function as it did. With less than 10,000 students in 1956–60, and with no new major programs or schools, no particular augmentation of line officers or official authority were needed. The officers did double duty by also acting as staff advisors to the Chancellor and as communications links to the departments and faculty. They were able to do this by vigorously using known and regularized channels of communication with the faculty, whose ranks they had left only recently and whose confidence they enjoyed. In other universities with more formalized bureaucracies of long standing, and particularly in the larger and more complex institutions, such doubling of staff and line functions would be impossible, and perhaps undesirable as well. Under different institutional conditions, more staff personnel would be necessary to collegialize line authority. Nevertheless, the UNC succession highlights the positive effect of collegialization, and the value of a strong staff component alongside lines of authority and

[10] This situation contradicts the ideas that disposing of the old lieutenants is always difficult and prolonged, and that new executives lack informal relations with the lower echelons. See Alvin Gouldner, "The Problem of Succession and Bureaucracy," *Studies in Leadership* (New York: Harper & Bros., 1950), pp. 654–5.

[11] For examination of pressures for goal achievement and the consequences thereof, see Oscar Grusky, "Managerial Succession and Organizational Effectiveness," *American Journal of Sociology*, LXIX (July 1963), 21–31; and Robert H. Guest, "Managerial Succession in Complex Organizations," *American Journal of Sociology*, LXVIII (July 1962), 47–56.

official communication that are fully used but sparingly extended.

The data on academic departments (Part IV) lend further support to the case for collegialized management. In the first place, the power of the departments in major universities makes them generic sources of management problems and of organizational strain. Departments must be reckoned with and attended, for they effectively control the quality of those professional services upon which, in turn, the reputation and future of any university depends in significant degree. In membership appeal and loyalty, the departments are potent social units, their uni-discipline nature being nicely suited to the values and needs of those specialized experts who constitute the university's faculty. Though they seldom initiate changes in general university policies, the departments often block such changes, and they may break the innovators as well. Their organizational structures and administrative processes are variable and unstandardized, and the culture of collegia are little known as yet to either analysts or administrators.

The classic bureaucracy of line authority and specialized officialdom was never designed to accommodate collegial groups, much less to enhance collegiality and professionalism. Yet, if universities are to achieve excellence, their management must accommodate the organization to its professional cadre, and see that the academicians' work is supported and stimulated in every way possible. For this to happen, top management on both the academic and business sides must relate co-operatively, and as directly as possible, with the academic departments through a formal structure that is kept as flat as possible. And the departments, through their chairmen (in the line of authority) and by means of faculty representatives on university committees (in staff-advisory connections), must be enabled to participate fully in important policy-making. The more effective their collegial collaborations, the less likely are the managers to apply truth strategies that are inappropriate or outdated. While it is true, as Thompson and his co-authors observe, that plural strategies tend to make management problems in universities, they also constitute a safeguard against inept academic management. Especially is this the case where plural strategies can be advocated through collegialized procedures of communication and decision-making and where, correspondingly, there is a management and faculty dialogue that includes important educational issues.

The managers of scientists and scholars, be they in universities or in other organizations, may well bear in mind Taylor's finding that the satisfactions of faculty were associated significantly with the good reputations of their departments. And these departments—all in distinguished universities—are likely to be more collegial and less bureaucratic in their structures of power and esteem than other kinds of groups, and than academic departments in lesser institutions. But, supposing the chairman, dean, or president remembers this finding, what is he to *do* on the basis of it? The satisfaction-reputation finding does present difficulties. From one point of view, it can be argued that high-satisfaction level is a result of good reputation and excellence of the university department. On the other hand, with equal cogency, it can be maintained that high satisfaction is a necessary precondition for achieving departmental eminence. The research man is apt to conclude that the two factors are probably interdependent, and there is no simple causal relationship between them. But the administrator, on the contrary, might draw a more pragmatic conclusion. Satisfaction of the faculty with conditions that are, in part, administratively manipulable may account for as much as 30 per cent of the variability in department excellence and reputation. This prospect merits careful attention in a market place that today and in the foreseeable future belongs in large part to the "sellers"—the academic professionals. To manipulate these not so obvious conditions and

233

interrelations of faculty satisfaction and dissatisfaction efficiently and with the desired effect, the university manager will need faculty collaboration—not just general demands and unsolicited advice.

Collegialized management can yield attractive dividends. Consider Taylor's nine satisfaction items presented in Chapter 11. Although the university manager may be unable to alter conditions affecting such things as "personal enjoyment" or "family satisfaction" in the local community, he can often change or contribute to changes in other respects: salary, opportunity for salary increase, requisites for good teaching and for scholarly achievement. Through administrative intervention in these matters, and as a consequence of style, the president, dean, chairman, business manager can affect the "department as a place to work" and even "social relations with department colleagues." Wherever the faculty think the managers can possibly affect faculty satisfactions, they will almost certainly be held responsible by the faculty for their deeds or inaction. And as we have seen in the succession at the University of North Carolina, the administrative style set at the top, and the deeds of top managers, do make a difference in satisfactions and excellence.

Finally, when the institution's interests compel intervention by managers in department affairs, or when department requests must be denied, already established collegialized procedures will be advantageous. As we have suggested earlier, the responsible academic manager occasionally must intervene in department affairs, even though his action may be unpopular and an objective evaluation difficult to make. To know who is who in the power and politics of the departments, and to know where individuals stand on the ladders of faculty esteem, is to be prepared and prudent in the delicate art of departmental intervention. Based on such knowledge, collegialized managers' interventions are more likely to be for good cause, from the organization's viewpoint as well as from the faculty's and the department's. And the method of intervening is more likely to be the right one.

SKETCH OF THE COLLEGIALIZED MANAGER

Although the presidents of universities are customarily "done" by painters in oil, no administrative scientist has portrayed verbally a collegialized president or top management. Nor have we the factual materials with which to draw a definitive verbal portrait. However, from Stephens' study of presidents, from the succession study of administrative style, from Taylor's survey of academic departments, and from other data presented, a preliminary outline or sketch can be drawn which reflects the facts as well as certain desiderata.

To begin with, the selection of the president will have been made with the participation of faculty representatives. And the selection procedure that was followed will probably have been more rational and efficient than boards of trustees commonly employ. That is, there will have been a representative faculty committee that advised the trustees committee in frequent joint meetings, which participated in interviews, and which agreed with the trustees committee on the names of all candidates recommended to the board for final action.[12] As the outcome of such a faculty-informed procedure, the president will probably be a "professor-administrant," or that rare figure, an academically sophisticated non-professor who is confident and comfortable in faculty society. Once in office, the president will have selected his immediate staff, and will have appointed deans and department chairmen, with the advice of appropriate faculty groups and individuals.

At work, the president will create and give leadership to a small team of top-line officials and staff assistants, several of

[12] These joint actions are included in the selection procedure outlined in fifteen recommendations by Frederick deW. Bolman, *How College Presidents Are Chosen* (Washington: American Council on Education, 1965), pp. 47–51.

235

whom will be his office neighbors. The collegialized president will have delegated as much responsibility and authority as possible for the roles of Money Man, Father Figure, Public-Relations Man, and Educator (before the public). A second, less closely related executive group—under a vice-president, perhaps—will have responsibility for business routines, facilities, and services to students and faculty. For himself, the president will take the role of academic general manager, and give it first priority personally and organizationally. In this role the deans and chairmen will be the collaborators of the president, who may be aided by a personal assistant or even a provost or vice-president to whom he has delegated more special tasks of academic management. The other roles and their respective executive assignments will be made to revolve around and give support to that of academic management, recognizing the centrality of education in its triangular form—research, teaching, and service.

However much time and effort goes to internal affairs, the president as academic general manager will not neglect the university's external relations insofar as their development and expansion contribute to the educational mission. The collegialized executive may well take up James A. Perkins' "hard if uncomfortable prescriptions," as noted in *The New York Times*:[13]

Instead of bemoaning the influence of Federal money, he challenges the universities to create huge regional, national and even international compacts of academic collaboration and planning. Isolated independence is an anachronism in an age when not even the strongest of the universities can pretend to cover the entire spectrum of knowledge or foot the bill for the huge cost of scientific inquiry. While it has been customary in the past for each university to admit only reluctantly that other universities also exist ("and then mainly for the purposes of arranging football sched-

[13] Editorial, "The Role of the University," *The New York Times*, November 8, 1965 (international edition). (President Perkins' lectures are to be published by the Princeton University Press in 1966.)

ules"), only a rapid move from autonomy to systems of higher education can *assure that ultimate decision-making will be in academic rather than political hands.* [Italics ours.]

But the collegialized manager will recognize that for universities to take the initiative in these matters is no guarantee that "ultimate decision-making will be in academic rather than political hands." After all, the decisions may be taken by bureaucratic officials in the universities who never taught a class or wrote a monograph; or, if they did once upon a time, may since have lost touch with collegium. Unless university management is collegialized, the decision may be distinctly non-academic, producing less rather than more internal cohesion, and evoking apathy or sabotage rather than collaboration from the faculty.

Collegiality begins at home with the daily encounters in the departments, the executive offices, the committee rooms, and faculty meetings. It is here that the executive, if collegialized, will develop an administrative style not unlike that observed in our study of succession at the top: (1) effective communication between faculty and executive; (2) identification with the faculty and their viable objectives; (3) orderly procedures vigorously utilized by hard-working officials, department chairmen included; and (4) collegial power facilitated by and joined with appropriate bureaucratic authority. Withal, the collegialized manager will accept the first maxim that Herman B. Wells, the distinguished one-time president of Indiana University, advised when he spoke of "How to Succeed as a University President without Really Trying."

Remind yourself daily that administration must always be the servant, never the master, of the academic community. It is not an end unto itself and exists only to further the academic enterprise. It follows, therefore, that the least administration possible is the best.[14]

[14] Herman B. Wells, "Points of View," *Bulletin of the International Association of Universities* (August 1965), p. 171.

Finally, the president will regularly check the satisfactions of the faculty, particularly those he can do something about. He may utilize research on his own institution, even to surveys like those represented in this book. Also, when careful evaluation shows it is necessary, the president, through his deans and chairmen, will intervene in departmental affairs. In doing so, however, he will have as full knowledge as possible of the collegial society and culture, its structures of power and esteem, and its truth strategies.

Put in jeopardy by bureaucratization of structure with its attendant rigidities and routines, the university can get out nevertheless. Collegialized management, we think, is the way out. Strong manager executives who institute orderly procedures for faculty participation will make collaboration possible between officials and faculty where, today, the divergence is dangerous and the choices appear to be either hyper-organization or "organizational dry rot."[15] The evidence is clear: collegialized management is the *sine qua non* of educational innovation and excellence in our universities.

[15] John W. Gardner's excellent thoughts on "organizational dry rot" and "continuous renewal" will be found in his article, "How to Prevent Organizational Dry Rot," *Harper's*, October 1965, pp. 20–6.

APPENDIX A

The Presidency: Power at the Top

NOTE ON METHOD OF RESEARCH

The presidency was viewed by Stephens as one position or office in university organizations—a position associated with a particular set of social norms, composing, in turn, a complex of social roles. It was postulated that in the presidential position, as in other positions, there is a strain toward consistency or adjustment between the various component roles. That is, it was assumed that inconsistent, contradictory, or maladjusted roles in a given position will evoke psychological tensions in the incumbent, who will then act to reduce these tensions.

A major methodological assumption of Stephens' presidency study was that historical and autobiographical documents by and about presidents, trustees, professors, and other university officials are capable of being converted into scientific data and applied to the exploration of presidential roles. It was assumed, further, that the autobiographical or personal writings reflect the normative aspects of the authors' orientations toward different situations— what the individual believes he is, or was, supposed to do, or what he perceives as appropriate behavior for the occupant of the presidency. The quantitative assessment of the incidence of these normative orientations and their interrelationships (by means of "content analysis," as explained in Stephens' dissertation) may be a useful preliminary to more definitive field studies of administrative relationships in universities. Literary products are no substitute for data collected by more systematic and reliable methods, such as the interview or direct observation of behavior. Moreover, it is recognized that many organizationally salient events and experiences of presidents cannot be published. Occasionally, inferences have been made on the basis of personal documents, the reader being warned appropriately. As any professional scholar knows well, the problems of sampling and analyzing such materials are numerous. Stephens' dissertation contains information on the sampling procedure and on the problems of validity, reliability, and quantification.

The data for the presidency study came from three main sources:

1. *Writings by presidents and writings by others about presidents and the presidency,* including biographies; autobiographies; letters; addresses; administrative reports; published pronouncements from conferences, congresses, and other meetings; and published articles and books pertaining to the presidency, to administrative processes and relationships, and to university objectives and aims.

2. *General texts, manuals, and directives* on the administration of universities and colleges, including formal descriptions of university organizations; listings of the duties and responsibilities formally assigned to occupants of the presidency and of other positions; and descriptions and explanations of formal reorganizations and of changes in administrative policies, objectives, or relationships.

3. *Governmental and other surveys and statistical studies* of universities and colleges—and studies utilizing these sources—including materials on occupants of the presidency and of other offices; on academic income and expenditure budgets; and on historical trends.

Other sources consulted were a number of historical works relating either to specific institutions or to university administration in general; and a number of studies pertaining either to the administration of professionals or to the behavior of executives in various nonacademic organizations.

A supplementary survey of 270 presidents, 1960–61, analyzed the backgrounds of presidents at eighty-eight major universities—with more than 5,000 students and which included the forty-five institutions studied earlier by Stephens in his doctoral research—plus the backgrounds of 182 other presidents. The sample of 182 was obtained by eliminating from a total of 1,892 the presidents of all those institutions of less than 5,000 students that were *not* classified as accredited universities or liberal-arts colleges by the U.S. Department of Education in 1960—institutions that include teachers' colleges, technical or professional schools, and junior colleges. Eliminated also were the presidents of Negro colleges, of women's colleges, and of institutions operated by the Roman Catholic Church. Our data are on age, prior occupation, education, and other background features, and were gathered principally from three sources: *Who's Who in America* (1960–61), *Leaders in American Education* (1961–62), and *Presidents and Deans of American Colleges and Universities* (1960–61). Table A–1 shows all 270 of the institutions in our double sample according to size, location, and type of control—public, private non-denominational, or private denominational. Tables A–2, A–3, and A–4 contain the data on presidents' backgrounds.

TABLE A–1

The Institutions of the 270 Presidents, by Region, Size of Enrollment, and Type of Control, 1960–61

Region	Over 5,000 Students*				Between 500 and 5,000 Students			
	Public	Private Non-denomi-na-tional	Private De-nomi-na-tional	Total	Public	Private Non-denomi-na-tional	Private De-nomi-na-tional	Total
Northeast	2	4	—	6	4	12	—	16
Middle Atlantic	7	11	2	20	3	13	23	39
Southeast	12	2	1	15	4	8	26	38
Midwest	17	5	1	23	9	9	32	50
Southwest	7	1	3	11	8	1	10	19
Rocky Mountain	3	—	1	4	4	2	1	7
West Coast	7	2	—	9	1	2	10	13
TOTALS	55	25	8	88	33	47	102	182

* Includes the forty-five selected universities whose presidencies are the main subject matter of Part II.

TABLE A–2

Occupational Experience of 270 Presidents, by Size
of Institution and Type of Control, 1960–61

Occupation before Presidency	Over 5,000 Students*				Between 500 and 5,000 Students			
	Public	Private Non-denominational	Private Denominational	Total	Public	Private Non-denominational	Private Denominational	Total
Professor	—	2	1	3	1	6	5	12
Academic Administrator†	2	—	—	2	1	2	5	8
Professor-Administrant	40	15	3	58	13	27	33	73
Public-school Admin.‡	5	2	2	9	12	1	9	22
Lawyer	3	1	1	5	1	1	1	3
Minister	2	1	1	4	1	2	32	35
Government or Politics	2	1	—	3	1	3	7	11
Business	—	1	—	1	1	—	6	7
Military	1	1	—	2	2	3	2	7
Foundation	—	1	—	1	—	—	2	2
Other	—	—	—	—	—	2	—	2
TOTALS	55	25	8	88	33	47	102	182

* Includes the forty-five selected universities.
† Includes deans, directors, and vice-presidents who were never professors.
‡ Includes public-school teachers.

TABLE A–3

Educational Achievement of 270 Presidents, by Size of Institution and Type of Control, 1960–61

Educational Achievement (highest degree)	Over 5,000 Students*				Between 500 and 5,000 Students			
	Public	Private Non-denomi-na-tional	Private De-nomi-na-tional	Total	Public	Private Non-denomi-na-tional	Private De-nomi-na-tional	Total
No degree earned	—	—	—	—	1	—	1	2
Bachelor's	4	6	1	11	2	3	18	23
Master's	16	3	2	21	4	12	31	47
Ph.D. or equivalent	32	16	5	53	17	29	44	90
Doctorate in Education	3	—	—	3	9	3	8	20
TOTALS	55	25	8	88	33	47	102	182

* Includes the forty-five selected universities.

TABLE A–4

Educational Specialization of 270 Presidents,
by Size of Institutions and Type of Control, 1960–61

Educational Specialization	Over 5,000 Students*				Between 500 and 5,000 Students			
	Public	Private Non-denominational	Private Denominational	Total	Public	Private Non-denominational	Private Denominational	Total
Humanities	6	3	2	11	2	7	9	18
Social science	19	6	1	26	6	13	18	37
Physical science	5	4	—	9	5	8	5	18
Education	10	1	—	11	11	4	14	29
Theology	1	1	4	6	1	3	39	43
Law	4	1	1	6	2	4	4	10
Engineering	5	1	—	6	3	5	—	8
Medicine	1	1	—	2	—	1	—	1
Administration (business/ government)	1	7	—	8	1	2	13	16
Agriculture	3	—	—	3	2	—	—	2
Other	—	—	—	—	—	—	—	—
TOTALS	55	25	8	88	33	47	102	182

* Includes the forty-five selected universities.

APPENDIX B

Administrative Style and Its Effects

THE IDEA of getting information from professors by means of a mail questionnaire on anything but questions directly affecting their own salaries, appointments, or promotions might seem a poor idea. And the more independent the faculty, perhaps the more foolhardy is the notion. Despite these misgivings, the questionnaire was devised and administered at the University of North Carolina in 1956. The response was surprising. From 506 voting (full-time assistant professors and up) members of the faculty, 318 replies were received—a return of 63 per cent. Used again in 1960, the questionnaire got a similar response. These replies represented a reliable cross-section of the faculty (see Table B–2) as judged by a number of criteria, including distribution among ranks, membership on the Faculty Council, membership in the AAUP, and distribution among the several academic divisions. The frequency, pungency, and pertinence of free comments, which in a number of instances ran over the space provided, showed that the responses were the product of thoughtful and interested consideration. The questionnaire success was attributable, we think, to several things: its brevity, the widespread interest in the subject matter, sponsorship by the Faculty Council, and, perhaps, the rationale on the face sheet.

MEMORANDUM

TO: All Faculty Members of the University at Chapel Hill

FROM: Faculty Council's "Committee on Faculty Action in University Government"

SUBJECT: FACULTY OPINION SURVEY

We do not like mimeographed mail, particularly questionnaires, any more than you do. However, this is the best way for us to get the information and advice we need on a problem of considerable importance to the University and to all of us, namely, the part played by the Faculty in UNC's government. The Faculty Council has recognized the importance of this problem in appointing our committee and in sponsoring this questionnaire.

Please strike out your name and address on the envelope enclosing this and return this questionnaire in it through interoffice mail to C. B. Robson, 101 Caldwell Hall, no later than February 15.

Please Follow These Instructions:

1. Do *not* sign your name; the questionnaire is entirely anonymous. We are interested only in complete reactions.

2. We want *your own* opinions and the facts as you see them. Please don't discuss any of the questions until *after* you have returned the questionnaire.

3. The space for Comments following most of the items is for you to give any elaboration you desire, after having checked the multiple-choice response. We have to rely on "yes-no" and other multiple-choice items so we can analyze the total results more easily, but we want anything else you care to say. A sheet is provided at the end of the questionnaire for general commentary and for continuations of any comments for which there may not have been enough room in the body of the questionnaire.

4. In connection with your Comments, we are interested especially in why you think this or that condition exists and *how* you believe it could be corrected or improved.

5. *Return* by February 15, and remember that the quality of our report to the Council will depend mostly on the candor and completeness with which the Faculty answers this questionnaire.

> With thanks for your cooperation,
> C. B. Robson (Chairman) (Political Science)
> N. J. Demerath (Sociology-Anthropology)
> G. M. Harper (English)
> E. C. Markham (Chemistry)
> S. Y. Tyree (Chemistry)
> A. M. Whitehill (Business Administration)

February 6, 1956   Committee on Faculty Action in University Government

FACULTY OPINION SURVEY

In accordance with the memorandum attached, please complete this questionnaire and return to Professor C. B. Robson, 101 Caldwell Hall, by February 15 at the latest.

I. *Background Information*

Please complete as many of these items as you care to, so we may better analyze all the questionnaire results. Any items you may hesitate to check for reaons of privacy, don't bother with. Again we remind you, however, that all replies are to be kept anonymous.

1. My academic rank is (CHECK ONE)
   1) __ Full-time Instructor
   2) __ Assistant Professor
   3) __ Associate Professor
   4) __ Professor
   5) __ Other (SPECIFY) _____

2. My department, professional school, or other University agency is (WRITE IN) _____

3. My age is (CHECK ONE)
   1) __ Under 30
   2) __ 31 to 40
   3) __ 41 to 50
   4) __ 51 to 60
   5) __ Over 60

4. During my academic career I have taught in __ colleges or universities. (INSERT THE NUMBER.)

5. I have been on the faculty at Chapel Hill (CHECK ONE)
   1) __ Less than 2 years
   2) __ 2 to 5 years
   3) __ 6 to 10 years
   4) __ 11 to 15 years
   5) __ 16 to 20 years
   6) __ More than 20 years

6. Are you *presently* a member of the Faculty Council? (CHECK ONE)
   1) __ Yes
   2) __ No

7. Have you *ever* been a member of the Faculty Council? (CHECK ONE)
   1) __ Yes
   2) __ No

8. Are you a member of the local chapter of the American Association of University Professors? (CHECK ONE)
   1) __ Yes
   2) __ No

9. Since September 1953, have you had contact with the Trustees' Visiting Committee? (CHECK ONE)
   1) __ Yes (HOW MANY TIMES?) __
   2) __ No
   COMMENTS:

10. Since September 1953, have you had contact, officially or unofficially, with a member of the board of trustees on matters of University business? (CHECK YES OR NO. IF YOU CHECK YES, PLEASE ANSWER "HOW MANY TIMES" AND "HOW MANY TRUSTEES.")
    1) __ No
    2) __ Yes
    3) *How many times?* __
    4) *How many different trustees?* __
    COMMENTS:

11. Of the committees, boards and councils listed on Page 2, write in the number you belong to at present, and the number you have belonged to since September 1953
    1) __ At present
    2) __ Total since September 1953

ADVISORY COMMITTEES OR GOVERNING BOARDS

Graduate School
Library
Division of Natural Sciences
Division of Social Sciences
Division of Humanities
Division of Health Affairs
   Medicine, Pharmacy, Nursing,
   Dental, Public Health, Hospital
Institute of Latin American Studies
Governors, University Press
Athletic Council
Business School
School of Education
School of Journalism

Law School
College of Arts and Sciences
General College
Summer Session
School of Library Science
School of Social Work
Institute for Research in the Social
   Sciences
Extension Division
Communication Center
Institute of Fisheries Research
Administrative Board of Student
   Affairs
Development Council

STANDING COMMITTEES OF THE FACULTY

Advisory
Established Lectures
Communication
Honorary Degrees
University Government
Catalog
Registration
Scholarships, Awards, and
   Student Aid
Faculty Welfare
Instructional Personnel
Athletics

Executive
English Composition
Examinations and Instruction
Radioisotopes
Admissions Policy
Fraternities and Sororities
Regulation of Dances
Sullivan Award
Retirement Arrangements
Buildings and Grounds
Plans and Projects

AD HOC COMMITTEES FOR THE CHANCELLOR

State of the University Conference
Carolina Symposium on Public Affairs
Management Survey and CM & P
   Report
French House
Medieval Center
Oak Ridge
Television Programming
Tobacco Research
Morehead Scholarship
Traffic
Marshall Scholarship
Rhodes Scholarship
Tanner Award Scholarship
Gardner Award
A & S Dean and General College Dean
Faculty Handbook
Kerr Dam
Security Clearance
University Stores
News Bureau
Medicinal Chemistry Meeting
General College Retarded Students
Librarian Selection

Committee on Physics Department
Atomic Energy Commission
Carolina-Duke Library
Graphic Arts
Middle East Studies
Radioisotope Laboratory
University Council on Undergraduate
   Education
Woodrow Wilson Scholarship
Fulbright
Jackson Scholarship
Residence Status
Special Sorority Problems
Ford Foundation Scholarship
School of Business Dean
Social Security Campaign
Group Insurance
Faculty Salaries
Use of Space
Ackland Building
Public Relations
Woodrow Wilson Centennial
Dean of Library Science
Dean of School of Education

II. *The Faculty's Part in Policy Formation*

The reference in each question is to the University *at Chapel Hill.*

12. On the average, how interested do you believe other faculty members are in matters concerning University policy?
(CHECK ONE)
    1) __ Very interested
    2) __ Moderately interested
    3) __ Uninterested
    COMMENTS:

13. Compared to others on the UNC faculty, do you consider yourself to be more, or less, interested in matters concerning University policy? (CHECK ONE)
    1) __ More interested than the average
    2) __ About as interested as average
    3) __ Less interested than the average
    COMMENTS:

14. To what extent do you feel that faculty opinion influences University-wide decisions concerning broad educational policy? (CHECK ONE) Faculty opinion is:
    1) __ Ignored
    2) __ Accorded minor importance
    3) __ Given moderate consideration
    4) __ Given substantial weight
    5) __ Decisive
    COMMENTS:

15. How do you feel about approaching the Trustees' Visiting Committee with your views concerning University government?
(CHECK ONE)
    1) __ I would never approach the committee
    2) __ I would be rather hesitant to approach the committee

    3) __ I would have no hesitancy in approaching the committee
    COMMENTS:

16. To what extent do you feel the "State of the University" conferences provide an effective medium for expressing faculty opinion? (CHECK ONE)
    1) __ Very effective
    2) __ Fairly effective
    3) __ Ineffective
    COMMENTS:

17. What do you think of the Faculty Council as an effective medium for expressing the faculty's viewpoints? (CHECK ONE)
    1) __ Very effective
    2) __ Fairly effective
    3) __ Ineffective
    COMMENTS:

18. Each Division of the University now selects representatives to the Faculty Council on a proportional basis. A specified number of representatives from each academic rank is elected by each Division from within its own membership. How representative do you think this is?
    1) __ Very representative
    2) __ Fairly representative
    3) __ Not representative
    COMMENTS:

19. Would you prefer that Faculty Council members be *nominated* by the Divisions—maintaining the present proportional representation by Division and rank—but be elected by the Faculty at large? (CHECK ONE)
    1) __ Yes
    2) __ No
    COMMENTS:

20. As an individual, do you believe you have had an adequate chance to make your views known to those in a position to determine University policy? (CHECK ONE)
1) __ Yes
2) __ No
COMMENTS:

21. Do you believe you have had an opportunity to become adequately informed on problems of University policy in which you have a pertinent interest?
(CHECK ONE)
1) __ Yes
2) __ No
If not, how do you think you could have been better informed?
COMMENTS:

22. Did you vote in these elections held during the first semester, 1955–56? (CHECK EACH ELECTION IN WHICH YOU VOTED.)
1) __ Faculty Council Membership
2) __ Advisory Committee Membership

23. If you voted in either of the elections noted above, how did you make up your mind? (CHECK ONE OR MORE)
1) __ Talked with colleagues in my department
2) __ Talked with colleagues in other departments
3) __ Looked at list of eligible faculty members
4) __ Other (SPECIFY) _____
COMMENTS:

24. Have you read these reports? (CHECK EACH REPORT YOU HAVE READ.)
1) __ President's 1955 Annual Report
2) __ 1955 State of University Conference

3) __ 1955 Trustees' Visiting Comm.
4) __ Other reports of Schools or Divisions (SPECIFY) _____
COMMENTS:

25. Under what conditions would you read more reports like those listed above? (SPECIFY)

26. In general, who would you say has the strongest voice in determining University policy at UNC? (RANK IN ORDER BY INSERTING 1, 2, 3, etc., BELOW.)
a) __ Trustees
b) __ President
c) __ Chancellor
d) __ Faculty
e) __ Alumni
f) __ Students
g) __ Other (SPECIFY) _____
h) __ Others (SPECIFY) _____
COMMENTS:

27. With whom do you discuss your views on University policies most frequently? (CHECK ONE)
1) __ Family members
2) __ Members of my department
3) __ Members of other departments
4) __ Administrative officers
5) __ Others (SPECIFY) _____
COMMENTS:

28. With which administrative officers, excluding department chairmen, have you had the most contacts? (PLEASE LIST THESE BY Name and Position IN ORDER OF FREQUENCY, THE MOST FREQUENTLY CONTACTED FIRST.)
1. _____
2. _____
3. _____
4. _____
COMMENTS:

III. *Faculty Influence in Specific Areas of University Policy*

For each of the areas of policy formulation *at Chapel Hill* listed below, evaluate present *faculty* influence as compared with that of other groups (e.g., administration, students, trustees, alumni). (CHECK *only one* COLUMN FOR EACH ITEM.)

Faculty Influence at UNC in	FAR TOO MUCH	TOO MUCH	ABOUT RIGHT	TOO LITTLE	FAR TOO LITTLE
29. Academic appointment is					
30. Academic promotion is					
31. Selection of department chairmen is					
32. Selection of deans is					
33. Selection of administrators other than dept. chairman and deans is					
34. Allocation of time and nature of professional duties is					
35. Student discipline is					
36. Admissions policy is					
37. Control of intercollegiate athletics is					
38. Budget making and adjustment is					
39. Guiding UNC's public relations activities is					
40. Planning of buildings and grounds is					

COMMENTS:

IV. *The Effectiveness of Committees, Councils, and Boards at Chapel Hill*

Please evaluate the work of the committees, councils and boards at Chapel Hill, listed on page 2, in each of the following respects. *Check the one answer* which most nearly expresses your opinion on each item. In the spaces for "Comments" cite any improvements you think desirable. If you have had committee, board, or council experience at Chapel Hill, consider these groups and their work. If not, draw on your indirect impressions as far as possible.

41. In the appointment or election of these bodies, it is my opinion that
    1) ___ Present methods are acceptable
    2) ___ More of these bodies should be *appointed*
    3) ___ More of these bodies should be *elected*
    COMMENTS:

42. As to the qualification of the members of these bodies, I believe they are
    1) ___ Very well qualified
    2) ___ Fairly well qualified
    3) ___ Poorly qualified
    COMMENTS:

43. With respect to the clear and/or specific statement of what is expected from these bodies by the agencies assigning responsibilities to them, I believe
    1) ___ The present situation is satisfactory
    2) ___ There is too little clarity and/or specificity
    3) ___ There is too much clarity and/or specificity
    COMMENTS:

44. With respect to the effective division of labor, internally, within these bodies, I believe they are
    1) ___ Very efficient
    2) ___ Fairly efficient
    3) ___ Inefficient
    COMMENTS:

45. With respect to the degree of overlap between the functions of different bodies, I believe there is
    1) ___ A great problem
    2) ___ Some problem
    3) ___ No problem at all
    COMMENTS:

46. The skills of the chairmen are
    1) ___ Very adequate
    2) ___ Fairly adequate
    3) ___ Require improvement in regard to (CHECK *One or More* OF THESE)
    a) ___ Planning work
    b) ___ Delegating or assigning work
    c) ___ Electing members' cooperation
    d) ___ Getting discussion by members
    e) ___ Getting group decisions
    f) ___ Reporting & following up results
    COMMENTS:

47. As for the importance of most committee work to the real education achievement of the University, I think it is
   1) __ Very important
   2) __ Fairly important
   3) __ Unimportant
   COMMENTS:

48. The flow of significant information, views, and opinions between administration and faculty at Chapel Hill is
   1) __ Entirely adequate
   2) __ Fairly adequate
   3) __ Inadequate
   COMMENTS:

49. The flow of significant information, views, and opinions between departments, divisions, and schools at Chapel Hill is
   1) __ Entirely adequate
   2) __ Fairly adequate
   3) __ Inadequate
   COMMENTS:

50. A "question and answer" session has been proposed for the Faculty Council, the idea being that selected administrative officers would come to certain pre-arranged Council meetings prepared to answer questions by faculty members. How do you view this idea?
   1) __ Very favorable
   2) __ Rather favorable
   3) __ Unfavorable
   COMMENTS:

51. Another proposal is that all committee reports to the Faculty Council be circulated in writing to Faculty Council members at least one week prior to a Council meeting at which they would then be discussed. As a member of the Faculty Council, would you be willing to read committee reports in advance, and come prepared for discussion?
   1) __ Yes
   2) __ No
   COMMENTS:

V. *Last—A General Evaluation*

Considered in relation to the over-all educational excellence of the University and compared with other universities you know. (CHECK ONE COLUMN FOR EACH ITEM)

	Current Status of UNC				
	VERY GOOD	GOOD	AVERAGE	POOR	VERY POOR
53. Scholarly achievement of faculty					
54. Quality of undergraduate education					
55. Quality of graduate & professional education					
56. Student extra-curricular life					
57. Administration					
58. Intramural athletic programs					
59. Intercollegiate athletic program					
60. Student government					
61. Public relations activities					

COMMENTS:

With reference to your own personal and professional needs, how do you rate these conditions at UNC?

	Current Status				
	VERY GOOD	GOOD	ADEQUATE	POOR	VERY POOR
62. Present salary					
63. Opportunity for promotion in salary in rank					
64. Requisites for good teaching					
65. Requisites for scholarly achievement					
66. Personal enjoyment of life in Chapel Hill					
67. Family satisfaction with the community					

COMMENTS:

TABLE B–2

Representativeness of University of North Carolina
Samples, by Rank and Division
Total Faculty Compared with Questionnaire Respondents

| | Per Cents 1956 | | Per Cents 1960 | |
	Sample N-318	Faculty N-517	Sample N-409	Faculty N-651
Division				
Humanities	18	18	17	17
Natural sciences	18	16	16	17
Social sciences & professions	33	30	29	26
Health professions	31	36	38	40
Academic Rank				
Professor	49	44	35	38
Associate professor	28	24	25	25
Assistant professor	19	20	23	23
Instructor	2	12	11	14
Other and "no answer"	2	—	6	—
Member, Faculty Council				
Yes	20	18*	15	15*
No	78	81	84	85
"No answer"	2	—	1	—
Member, AAUP Chapter				
Yes	34	30*	21	32*
No	65	70	78	68
"No answer"	1	—	1	—

* The number on the Faculty Council was 95 in 1956, and 100 in 1960. The number belonging to the American Association of University Professors Chapter was 155 in 1956, and 210 in 1960.

APPENDIX C

The Academic Departments: Power and Reputation

THE QUESTIONNAIRE AND ITS ADMINISTRATION

The thirty departments that Taylor surveyed were chosen in the following manner. First, all "arts and sciences" departments at Chicago, Northwestern, Indiana, Cornell, and Pennsylvania were categorized by numbers of faculty into four size groups. Second, they were grouped according to disciplines (humanities, natural sciences, and social sciences). Then, by rolling dice, three from each of the twelve categories were chosen at random.

Next, a letter was sent to each department chairman, reminding him that his university was one of those participating in the Faculty Mobility Study (by Caplow and McGee), sponsored by the Fund for the Advancement of Education, and solicited his help in this study of departmental organization and administration. Each chairman was also sent a roster of his department's members as listed in the current university catalogue. He was asked to amend this roster to include all full-time staff members currently on the campus, and to return the amended roster for preparation of the questionnaires and the mailing list. Six departments did not reply in time to be included in the sample, and thus thirty instead of thirty-six departments were analyzed. In size of faculty staff, the departments ranged from twenty-nine to five, with a mean size of 13.5. The accuracy of the rosters was verified, and errors were corrected in several instances.

After a pilot study in a university not included in the survey, the questionnaires were mailed during the second week of May 1957 to all members of the thirty departments participating in the study. With this mailing went a covering letter, a stamped and addressed return envelope, and an instruction sheet to guide the respondent in completing the questionnaire. A follow-up postcard went to the entire mailing list one week later.

The questionnaire itself began with a face sheet containing questions on the respondent's age, academic rank, length of service, and similar matters. Then, with a separate page for each area, came the fourteen areas of departmental policy or action as noted in Chapter 10. On each page was an alphabetical list of the faculty roster for the recipient's own department. The recipient was asked to rate each member of his department according to whether he had a proportional (P), more than proportional (M), or less than proportional (L) *amount of "say" or influence* in the decisions affecting policy and action in the area. The sixteenth page asked the respondent to indicate the five policy areas of the fourteen which he considered to be the most important for the successful operation of a university department.

Page 17 of the questionnaire presented a list of ten items in the "departmental environment" with respect to which the respondent was asked whether *conditions of professional and personal life* were very good, good, average, poor, or very poor. These items were drawn mainly from the faculty-satisfaction index that had first been used in the University of North Carolina Faculty Opinion Survey, as reported in Part III of this book. On the same page the respondent was asked to indicate whether his department—as compared with other departments in the same field at other major universities—had a reputation as being (1) among the first five, (2) better than the average of major universities, (3) average, (4) poorer than the average of major universities.

Finally, on the last page of the questionnaire, the respondent was again presented with a roster of his departmental membership and was asked to indicate, for each member, whether he made a proportional, more than proportional, or less than proportional contribution to the *intellectual climate* of the department. These ratings, when pooled for respondents, served to provide "esteem" scores for each member of the departmental staff.

Table C-1

Frequency of Questionnaire Return, by Rank and Department

Dept.	Professors Sent	Professors Return	Assoc. Prof. Sent	Assoc. Prof. Return	Asst. Prof. Sent	Asst. Prof. Return	Instructors Sent	Instructors Return	Others Sent	Others Return	Total Sent	Total Return
Natural Sciences												
NS-A	1	1	1	1	3	3	0	0	0	0	5	5
NS-B	2	1	2	2	1	0	0	0	2	2	7	5
NS-C	2	2	1	1	4	3	1	1	0	0	8	7
NS-D	3	2	2	2	3	2	0	0	0	0	8	6
NS-E	5	3	4	0	5	3	1	0	0	0	15	6
NS-F	7	4	3	3	5	3	1	1	1	0	17	11
NS-G	5	3	7	5	3	3	2	0	4	2	21	13
NS-H	14	7	4	1	4	2	1	1	2	0	25	11
NS-I	12	4	5	2	9	3	2	1	1	0	29	10
Social Sciences												
SS-A	3	3	1	2	1	0	1	1	0	0	6	6
SS-B	3	2	1	0	2	2	1	0	0	0	6	6
SS-C	6	1	2	1	0	1	1	0	0	0	9	3
SS-D	6	3	2	2	0	0	0	0	2	1	10	6
SS-E	3	2	2	1	5	3	2	1	0	0	12	7
SS-F	7	4	2	2	2	1	1	0	0	0	12	7
SS-G	6	2	3	0	3	2	0	0	1	0	13	4
SS-H	6	4	5	2	4	2	1	0	0	0	16	8
SS-I	4	3	4	2	7	4	2	2	2	0	19	11
SS-J	4	0	5	2	6	4	4	3	0	0	19	9
SS-K	9	4	5	2	9	7	1	1	2	0	26	14

Dept.	Professors Sent	Professors Return	Assoc. Prof. Sent	Assoc. Prof. Return	Asst. Prof. Sent	Asst. Prof. Return	Instructors Sent	Instructors Return	Others Sent	Others Return	Total Sent	Total Return
Humanities												
H-A	3	1	0	0	2	1	0	0	1	1	6	3
H-B	5	2	1	0	1	0	0	0	0	0	7	2
H-C	3	2	1	0	2	0	2	1	0	0	8	3
H-D	6	3	4	2	1	1	0	0	0	1	11	7
H-E	4	2	2	1	2	0	2	2	1	0	11	5
H-F	4	1	3	2	0	0	5	4	0	0	12	7
H-G	8	1	2	1	3	1	0	0	0	0	13	3
H-H	7	3	2	0	5	3	1	1	0	1	15	8
H-I	6	3	6	4	5	5	1	0	1	0	19	12
H-J	9	3	5	2	2	1	4	2	0	0	20	8
TOTAL	163	76	87	45	99	60	37	22	20	8	406	211

NOTE: In four cases, the number in a "return" cell is larger than the corresponding number sent. Here we have (1) a shift in status, (2) a case of a questionnaire's being returned by a teaching assistant, or (3) a respondent who classified himself as "other," despite the fact that he holds a title that would call for him to be listed in another category, in which he was counted in the "sent" column.

About 52 per cent of the questionnaires mailed were returned in usably complete form. This percentage of return is satisfactory, but we believe the return would have been better had we not used bulk-rate postal service. Another obstacle to a higher return rate was the length of time required to complete the questionnaire, particularly in the larger departments with rosters including as many as twenty-nine names. The questionnaires used in the pilot study, which did not require a response to each name on the roster, took about twenty minutes to complete, on the average. It is likely that the survey's respondents may have taken up to twice as long to complete these questionnaires.

Only one man, to our knowledge, objected to the questionnaire and the study: a department chairman who had previously corrected and returned his departmental roster. He stated that he considered some of the questions on policy decisions "potentially dangerous," and asked about Taylor's credentials and the legitimacy of the study. We reflected privately that if mention of the policy matters was "potentially dangerous," these were surely important in department operations.

General comments were invited. Several respondents requested that the findings be made available to them in return for their cooperation in completing the questionnaire. Some wondered about the accuracy of their own responses; several were new members of the departments. Others expressed reservations about the over-all validity of the findings.

REPRESENTATIVENESS OF THE SAMPLE

Taking the 211 returns, 52 per cent of the 406 questionnaires mailed to the members of the thirty departments, how representative are the 211 of the 406? The random choice of departments, after they were stratified by size and subject matter, could be vitiated and the data distorted by a consistent tendency for certain viewpoints to be underrepresented or overrepresented in the responses of those who completed and returned the questionnaire.

Critical information on rank (and age, indirectly) is presented in Table C–1. In Table C–2 these figures are arranged more simply by indicating the frequency of response and non-response for each academic rank. We see that 47 per cent of professors (76 out of 163) returned their questionnaires; 52 per cent of associate professors (45 out of 87); 61 per cent of assistant professors (60 out of 99); and 57 per cent of instructors (22 out of 37). Is there something behind this pattern of response other than sheer chance?

TABLE C–2

Frequency of Questionnaire Return by Rank

	Respondents	Non-Respondents	Total
Professors	76	87	163
Associate professors	45	42	87
Assistant professors	60	39	99
Instructors	22	15	37
Other	8	12	20
TOTAL	211	195	406

SOURCE: Table B–2.

$X^2(4 \text{ d.f.}) = 6.7887; .2 \text{ p. } .1$

Excluding the catch-all category "other," we see that the professors had the lowest percentage of respondents, and the associate professors the next lowest response rate, while the assistant professors and instructors responded at similar rates, both of these being higher than those of the professors and associate professors. A chi-square test, noted at the bottom of Table C–2, indicates that these differences in responses might be attributable to chance in no more than 10 to 20 instances in 100.

To some extent, then, our data were provided disproportionately by the younger and lower rank faculty, who had had less time to learn the ways of their departments. However, time is not the only factor in learning, and the younger men in lower ranks may well be more astute and knowledgeable by virtue of their age-rank vantage points. Had the data provided by the 52 per cent response of the original mailing list been biased in the opposite direction, we might have less cause for concern, but then we do not know.

The rates of response can be analyzed in another way, comparing one department with another. Referring again to Table C–1, we find a somewhat greater variation than in the rank-by-rank approach. In two of the smaller departments (NS-A and SS-A) we find 100 per cent of the membership returning questionnaires. At the other extreme (department H-B), we find as few as two out of seven members returning questionnaires. Inasmuch as a small

TABLE C-3

Power and Esteem Ratings of Thirty Department Chairmen

Department	Size	Power Range	Chairman's Power	Esteem Range	Chairman's Esteem	Rank on Esteem*
Natural Sciences						
NS-A	5	31–114	114	4– 9	4	5th (last)
NS-B	7	6–132	132	3– 8	4	5th
NS-C	8	24–170	170	2–12	11	2nd
NS-D	8	45–126	126	0–12	12	1st
NS-E	15	28–150	150	0–11	5	3-tie for 7th
NS-F	17	32–283	283	5–18	18	1st
NS-G	21	12–310	310	0–24	11	11th
NS-H	25	60–258	258	3–19	16	4th
NS-I	29	28–217	217	1–18	9	4-tie for 16th
Social Sciences						
SS-A	6	15–144	144	2–11	4	5th
SS-B	7	25– 87	87	3– 5	5	3-tie for 1st
SS-C	9	15– 75	75	0– 6	2	2-tie for 5th
SS-D	10	18–132	132	3– 8	7	4th
SS-E	12	24–177	177	0–10	5	9th
SS-F	12	12–184	184	0– 8	7	2-tie for 2nd

Department	Size	Power Range	Chairman's Power	Esteem Range	Chairman's Esteem	Rank on Esteem*
SS-G	13	14– 96	96	1– 7	7	3-tie for 1st
SS-H	16	27–231	231	1–18	1	2-tie for last
SS-I	19	13–282	282	1–14	13	2-tie for 2nd
SS-J	19	12–236	236	1–18	11	3-tie for 5th
SS-K	26	32–302	302	2–27	23	5th
Humanities						
H-A	6	6– 79	79	0– 6	5	3rd
H-B	7	12– 45	45	1– 3	3	3-tie for 1st
H-C	8	10– 76	76	0– 6	5	3-tie for 3rd
H-D	11	30–172	172	1–12	12	1st
H-E	11	3–134	134	0–10	5	3-tie for 5th
H-F	12	5–179	179	1–14	6	5th
H-G	13	14– 70	70	0– 4	3	4-tie for 3rd
H-H	15	29–195	195	3–14	9	8th
H-I	19	48–277	277	3–16	16	2-tie for 1st
H-J	20	21–222	222	2–15	13	2-tie for 4th

* In the "Rank on Esteem" column, entries are to be read as follows: for "3-tie for 7th," read, "3-way tie for 7th place." The underlined entries in this column indicate rank positions at or below the median rank for the department; i.e., underlined entries indicate chairmen falling in the lower half of the esteem hierarchy in their departments.

number of respondents may produce relatively unstable scores for their department on the various measures employed in our analysis, the reader should note the following five departments as ones in which fewer than four members returned their questionnaires: H-B, SS-C, H-G, H-A, and H-C.

As the questionnaires were returned, they were edited where necessary to render them comparable with one another. In the few instances where a policy-area page was left blank, each name on the roster was assigned a "proportional" rating of his influence in that area. In other cases where some of the names on a page were not rated, these blanks were filled in by "proportional" ratings insofar as this was not inconsistent with a general rule applied to all returns. According to this rule, if at least one member of a department was rated by a respondent as being more than proportionally influential in a policy area, at least one other member of the department must have been rated by that respondent as less than proportionally influential in that area. The rule was also applied in reverse. That is, if one or more men received less than proportional ratings, at least one member must also have been rated as more than proportionally influential by that respondent.

Further details of the survey, its concepts and methods, will be found in Taylor's monograph, already cited. Three tables of data, basic to much of the interpretation of Chapter 10 and 11, conclude this Appendix.

TABLE C–4

Number of Chairmen in Top Power-Position, by Importance of Policy Area

Policy Area	Respondents Rating the Policy Area as among Five Most Important Areas	Chairmen in Top Power-Position on the Policy Area
1. Appointments to the departmental faculty	195	17
2. Planning and revision of departmental curriculum	137	13
3. Advance in rank of a faculty member	114	17
4. Support of research activities of the members of the departmental faculty	141	15
5. Vocational placement of students	28	15
6. Salary advancement for a faculty member	80	27
7. Handling the public relations of the department	17	23
8. Recruiting of students, both undergraduate and graduate, to major in the department	109	15
9. Planning and revision of the departmental budget	47	29
10. Handling the relations of the department with other parts of the university system	43	26
11. Selection of a new departmental chairman (hypothetically or in recent past)	61	11
12. Assignment of graduate assistants to specific responsibilities or supervisors	9	18
13. Allocation of specific courses to individual faculty members	25	25
14. Appointments to committees of the department	5	26

Table C-5

Three Characteristics of Thirty Departmental Structures[*]

Department	Power-Esteem Correlation −1 to +1	Equalitarianism 0 to 1	Monomorphism 0 to 1
Natural Sciences			
NS-A	−.07	.39	.57
NS-B	−.09	.32	.93
NS-C	.42	.29	.75
NS-D	.79	.53	.55
NS-E	.33	.41	.58
NS-F	.38	.26	.68
NS-G	.80	.34	.92
NS-H	.23	.52	.67
NS-I	.43	.38	.80
Social Sciences			
SS-A	−.00	.31	.79
SS-B	.36	.49	.59
SS-C	.21	.36	.53
SS-D	.68	.33	.83
SS-E	.16	.41	.59
SS-F	.71	.26	.76
SS-G	.85	.31	.77
SS-H	.20	.31	.74
SS-I	.66	.29	.82
SS-J	.71	.34	.83
SS-K	.72	.29	.78
Humanities			
H-A	.52	.31	.74
H-B	.65	.47	.57
H-C	.35	.20	.60
H-D	.86	.35	.80
H-E	.80	.28	.90
H-F	.58	.21	.90
H-G	.55	.40	.64
H-H	.80	.33	.74
H-I	.59	.44	.70
H-J	.87	.28	.62

[*] Entries rounded to two decimal places. Prior computations were with figures rounded to four decimal places.

INDEX